# A DAY THAT MADE HISTORY

# THE ARMADA:
## THE DECISIVE BATTLE

Nathaniel Harris

Dryad Press Limited   London

# Contents

## THE EVENTS

## THE INVESTIGATION

## Acknowledgments

The author and publishers thank the following for their kind permission to reproduce copyright illustrations: BBC Hulton Picture Library, page 33; Blandford Press, pages 8, 13; Bodleian Library, Oxford, page 20; the British Library, page 50; Courtauld Institute, pages 58, 60; Mansell Collection, page 37; Museo Naval, Madrid, page 12; National Maritime Museum, pages 5, 6, 7, 11, 15 (left), 22, 24, 35 (right), 36, 52-3, 61; National Portrait Gallery, London, pages 15 (right), 48, 62; Photographie Giraudon, page 44; Public Record Office, page 51; Rijksmuseum, Amsterdam, page 47; Saint Faith's Church, King's Lynn, page 34; Society of Apothecaries, cover; Victoria and Albert Museum, page 35 (left). The photograph on page 43 is reproduced by gracious permission of Her Majesty the Queen. The photograph on page 4 is reproduced by kind permission of the Marquess of Tavistock and the Trustees of the Bedford Estates. The map on page 46 was drawn by R.F. Brien. The pictures were researched by David Pratt.

The "Day that Made History" series was devised by Nathaniel Harris.

Typeset by Tek-Art Ltd, Kent, and printed by R.J. Acford, Chichester, Sussex for the publishers, Dryad Press Limited, 8 Cavendish Square, London W1M 0AJ

ISBN 0 8521 9686 5

# THE
# EVENTS

## The night of the fireships

### *Confrontation*

On Sunday, 7th August, 1588, two hostile fleets lay within
cannon-shot of each other in the English Channel, just off the
French coast. The Spaniards were anchored close to the cliffs
of Calais; the English stood out to sea, ready to stalk or
pounce on their enemies. The Spanish fleet was the great
Armada, sent by King Philip II on "the Enterprise of
England" – the name the Spaniards gave to their intended
invasion and conquest of Queen Elizabeth's realm; if it
succeeded, the heretical Queen was to be deposed and her
Protestant people forcibly converted to Catholicism. It was
the mission of the English fleet to prevent the Spanish ships
from landing and, if possible, to engage and destroy them.

In total, there were around two hundred and sixty English
and Spanish vessels facing one another on that Sunday. The
number of really effective fighting ships was smaller – perhaps
forty on each side – since the fleets included many patrol boats
and, on the Spanish side, hulks (troop transports and supply
ships); but even so there had never before been two such
fleets of sailing ships locked in combat. Europeans were used
to conflicts involving large numbers of warships, but these
were galleys propelled by oars and mainly operating in coastal
waters or the tideless Mediterranean. Fighting between
galleys was less a matter of seamanship than of soldiering.
They did battle by grappling – seizing enemy vessels by means
of hooking devices called grapnels, which the crewmen flung
across the spaces between the ships. This enabled troops
stationed on a galley to board the enemy and "conquer" him,
very much in the style of a land battle. But by 1588 the ocean-
going sailing ship had been developed into a new kind of war
weapon: the galleon. The cargo deck of this fast,

manoeuvrable vessel was lined with cannon that were capable of delivering devastating volleys of broadsides (that is, shots fired from the sides rather than the bow or stern of the ship). Although the Spaniards were slow to grasp the fact, soldiers now had no place in sea battles, which would be decided for the next few hundred years by duels between lethally armed sailing ships.

The English were experienced in this newer kind of combat, since Sir Francis Drake and other "sea-dogs" had been preying on Spanish shipping for years, using their galleons to wage an unofficial and profitable war on Spain. But in fights of this sort, only a few vessels were involved; it was still not clear what an encounter between large fleets would be like. And so it was that during the week of Sunday, 31st July, the English and Spanish fought the first engagements in history between fleets of sailing warships.

The results of this running fight up the Channel were not what either side had hoped for. The Spaniards' old-fashioned attempts to grapple and board had never looked like succeeding: English seamanship was too good. But although the English ships had proved themselves faster than the

*The commemorative "Armada portrait" of Queen Elizabeth I. The crown, the globe showing the Spanish Main, and the ships in the background create a picture-story of the struggle at sea.*

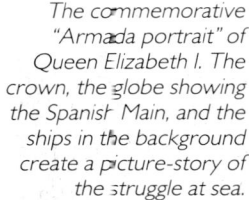

Spaniards' and superior in fire-power, the actual damage inflicted on the Armada had been disappointingly small. The Spaniards had lost only three vessels, and were still together and drawn up in close fighting order. Since even the best seamen were at the mercy of the weather, it was still quite possible that the Armada would manage to slip away and land a Spanish army somewhere on the English coast. The English Lord High Admiral, Howard of Effingham, could not yet be certain of victory.

The problems of the Spanish commander, the Duke of Medina Sidonia, were even more serious. Although the Armada was carrying nearly 19,000 fighting men, the bulk of the invasion force was supposed to consist of crack troops supplied by the Duke of Parma, the Spanish commander in the Netherlands. The Armada had in fact crossed the

*King Philip II of Spain, ruler of a vast empire and champion of Catholicism. He launched the Armada against England, hoping to destroy the chief support of European Protestantism and anti-Spanish rebellions.*

Channel in order to pick up Parma's men, who were to leave from Dunkirk in flat-bottomed barges which the Spanish fleet would escort to England. But now, despite frantic messages from Sidonia, Parma seemed unwilling to move into action.

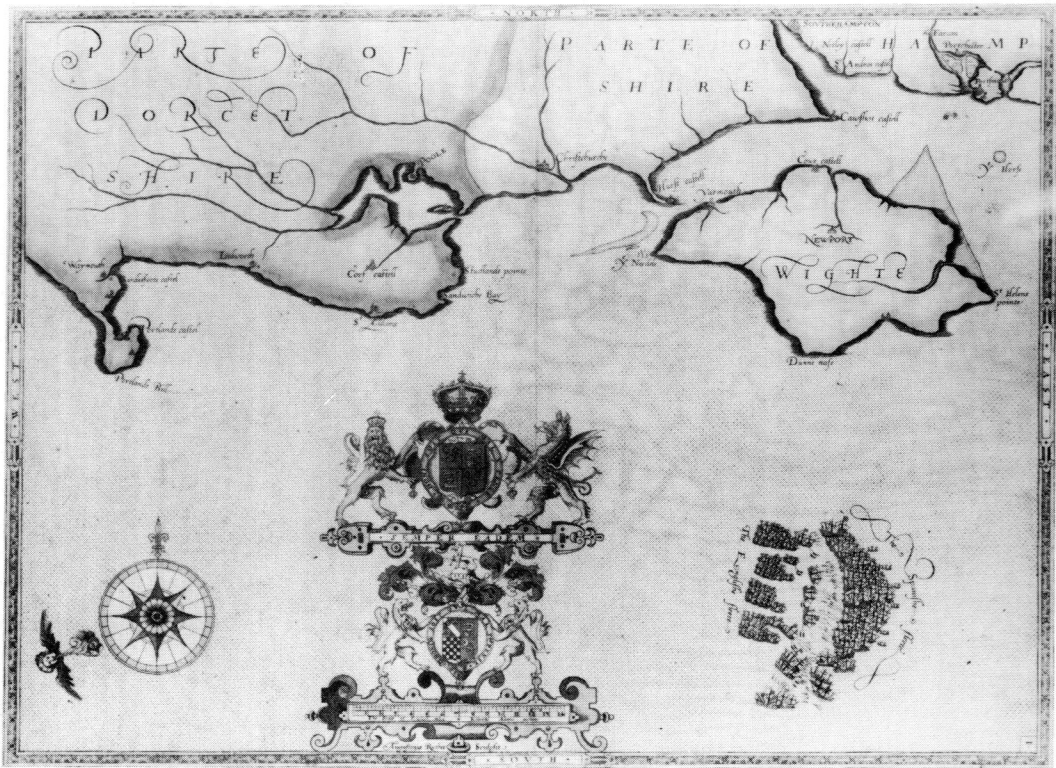

Until he did so, the Armada would have to remain in Calais Roads (the roadstead, or anchorage, outside Calais), offering a more or less stationary target for any English attack. Calais itself was closed to the Spaniards, since it was neutral French territory. And, to make matters worse, the Spaniards had almost exhausted their supplies of ammunition.

English supplies had also run low. Neither side had anticipated the vast quantities of powder and shot that would be used in the new kind of naval warfare. But the English had the great advantage of being close to their home base, and over the weekend they were sent new supplies of ammunition and victuals. They were also reinforced on the Saturday afternoon, when Lord Henry Seymour arrived with a squadron of vessels that had been patrolling the Downs. Some of the finest and newest of the Queen's ships were among them. The entire English fleet – some 140 vessels – was now present, outnumbering the 120-strong Armada. It was evidently the moment to make a decision, and early in the morning of Sunday, 7th August Howard put out the flag of council, summoning his chief officers to a conference on board his flagship, the *Ark*.

◁ *The fighting ships of the Armada, drawn up in their characteristic crescent formation, confront their English enemies; the Spanish supply ships and troop transports are positioned safely behind them. This is an eighteenth-century engraving made from a tapestry worked soon after the Armada campaign.*

◁ *The English and Spanish fleets engaged off the Isle of Wight. This was the first major action of the Armada campaign. English seamanship showed to advantage in it, but the outcome was indecisive, and afterwards the Armada sailed on unbroken. The map is one of a series, engraved by Augustine Ryther and published in 1590.*

*Charles Howard, Baron Effingham and Lord High Admiral of the English fleet.*

*The Ark, flagship of the English fleet. Compare her slender, trim appearance with the bulk of the San Martin (page 13). The drawing is a modern reconstruction by Ray Woodward.*

## "The device of fireworks"

Howard's council of war agreed that it was important to disturb the Spanish battle order and, if possible, prise the Armada out of its relatively protected position. To do so, they decided to use a tried and trusted weapon: fireships.

The fireship was just what its name suggested: a vessel packed with inflammable materials and set on fire. When directed against an enemy's fleet, fireships were unnerving – especially when used at night – and also potentially lethal, since fire was a terrible hazard for warships constructed of timber and stocked up with gunpowder. Vessels on the move could usually slip out of the way of oncoming fireships, but a fleet at anchor and in close formation – like the Armada – might well find successful evasive action impossible.

As soon as the decision was made, an officer named Sir Henry Palmer was sent in a pinnace (a light craft used for scouting and similar purposes) to collect the fireships that lay in readiness at Dover. But during the course of the day it became apparent that Palmer might not be back in time: if the wind changed or the Armada got under weigh, the chance to throw the enemy into confusion would have been missed. The only way to carry out the fireship plan was to sacrifice some of the ships in the fleet itself; and when volunteers were called for, eight captains came forward to offer their vessels. As a result of this decision, the English fireships were bigger than any that had ever been used before; and this was to have a significant effect on the action that followed.

Hoping to take the Spaniards by surprise, the English waited until darkness had fallen before beginning their preparations. Then the eight fireships were packed with anything that would burn – items such as spare timbers, ropes, lamp oil, and firewood used in the ships' galleys (kitchens). The masts and rigging were daubed with tar. And the ships' guns were double-loaded so that they would go off, adding to the Spaniards' confusion, when the heat on the burning vessels became intense. A West Country sailor, Captain John Young, was put in charge of the skeleton crews that would man the fireships until the last moment, and five small boats were allocated to take them off when their task was done.

These preparations were successfully concealed from the Spaniards, but it would not be true to say that the English took them by surprise. The use of fireships was a well-known tactic which Medina Sidonia expected the English to adopt; and he took intelligent defensive measures to deal with it. A number of pinnaces were detailed to form a screen in front of the fleet; their job was to intercept the fireships, seize them with grapnels, and steer them away from the Spanish vessels and on to the French coast. Medina Sidonia set out his plan in a message to the fleet urging his men not to panic. If the pinnaces failed to divert some of the fireships, the Spanish vessels were to have their own boats lowered so that these could fend off the intruders. And if all else failed, the Spanish captains were authorized to slip their cables, leave their anchorages, and stand out to sea until the danger was past; then they were to return straight away to their former stations. On the following morning, provided that at least one of the Duke's plans worked, the English would find the Armada untouched, still drawn up in close battle order outside Calais, and with the morale of its sailors and fighting men unshaken.

But there was another, unspoken danger that preyed on the Spaniards' minds. Medina Sidonia never referred to it officially until afterwards; he seems to have thought that his men were not aware of it, and concluded that there was no point in spreading alarm and despondency by mentioning it as a possibility. This dreadful danger was that the English might use Europe's latest and most destructive weapon – "hellburners". These were fireships with a difference: instead of merely burning, they exploded like missiles, with devastating results. (They were probably packed with large quantities of gunpowder, perhaps with the addition of iron bars so that they "went off" with a metal-hail effect, like grenades.) The hellburner was invented by an Italian engineer named Federigo Giambelli, and had so far been used only once: at the siege of Antwerp in 1585, when it had smashed the Spanish boom across the River Scheldt, flinging burning debris over an area a kilometre and a half wide and killing about a thousand of Parma's troops at a stroke. In sixteenth-century terms this was an appalling massacre: fewer men died in most of the battles Parma had fought. And now there were rumours that Giambelli was working for Queen Elizabeth in London, doubtless devising new weapons for use against England's enemies. The rumours were correct: Giambelli *was* in London, although he was in fact peacefully employed on the construction of a boom across the Thames to bar the passage of the Armada. But the terror his name inspired was to influence the events that followed.

### The scattering of the Spaniards

At about midnight, a gun on one of the English ships gave the signal for action. The skeleton crews set their vessels on course before firing them and hastily disembarking into the waiting boats. With a fresh breeze behind them and the tide flowing strongly towards the shore, the fireships bore down on the Armada at a speed that made any effective counter-action extremely difficult. Captain Young's men had done their work well. As the fires flared and then ran rapidly along the rigging, the Spaniards counted two, then eight tall ships racing towards them, so close together and regularly aligned that they gave the impression that they might still be carrying crews. They were also very much bigger than the Spaniards expected, and this may well have encouraged fears that they were hellburners or some other kind of infernal machine.

*Fireships launched towards the Spanish fleet around midnight on Sunday, 7th-8th August. This painting by an unknown contemporary artist depicts the crucial action that broke the Armada's formation.*

More immediately important was the fact that the fireships' size created problems for the Spanish pinnaces, which were much smaller than the vessels they were supposed to intercept, divert and tow away. And the fireships were so close to one another that the pinnaces could only tackle them side on, in an attempt to pull them away in twos, one from each end of the line. There was all too little time for such a series of operations, and in the event only two of the pinnaces were successful. The next two approached at the moment when the temperature on the gundecks reached white heat and the guns began to go off in all directions.

The shock caused by the explosions was sufficient to check the pinnaces and bewilder their crews for a moment – long enough to allow the remaining six fireships to pass them and sweep on towards the fleet in its anchorage. The explosions also served to convince the Spaniards that these were indeed the terrible hellburners of Antwerp, capable of blowing them all to Kingdom Come. The Duke of Medina Sidonia admitted to sharing the fears of his men when he later explained, in a letter to his royal master, that "fearing they [the English fireships] might contain fire machines or mines", he had commanded his crew to let go the cables of the flagship. He sent similar orders to the rest of the Armada, and a general evacuation of the anchorage began.

By mentioning his fear of "fire machines or mines" as a specific reason for moving, Medina Sidonia seemed to imply that the fireships in themselves presented no great danger – provided they *were* fireships, and not hellburners. Yet they were certainly too big to be warded off by men in ships' boats, as the Duke had instructed. Perhaps, after all, the fireships were not quite on target, and were unlikely to do much harm. If this was so, then the Duke's decision to leave the anchorage turned out to be disastrous, however understandable it may have been in the face of the oncoming English ghost ships that blazed and showered sparks and scattered shots about in the darkness of the night. The Spanish sailors had to work fast, since the fireships were almost upon them; patriotic English writers have often described this as a panic, but there seems no reason to suppose that the crews were anything but speedy and efficient. They slashed through the anchor cables with axes, set sail, and cleared the anchorage in the dark with only one serious collision in a fleet of 120 vessels. The six fireships passed harmlessly across Calais Roads and burned themselves out on the shore. They had not damaged a single Spanish ship; but they had accomplished something more important in scattering the Spanish fleet.

Medina Sidonia carried out his own instructions to the letter: his flagship, the *San Martin*, stood out to sea, dropping another anchor, until the tide turned and she was able to return to a station not far from her original anchorage. But when day broke there were only four other Spanish galleons in sight, though luckily for the Duke they were some of his best fighting ships. One, the *San Juan*, was commanded by the most experienced of living Spanish captains, the aged Juan Martinez de Recalde, who was serving as vice-admiral to the aristocratic Medina Sidonia; the others were the *Rata Encoronada*, commanded by the most distinguished military man in the fleet, Don Alonzo de Leyva, and two Portuguese galleons from the Duke's own squadron. (Philip II was King of Spain *and* Portugal; and the "Spanish Armada" was in reality a joint expedition.) The rest of the fleet had run before the wind and was now dispersed all along the coast as far as the village of Gravelines, about 15 kilometres west-north-west of Calais. The captains of the scattered vessels had probably no choice but to go with the wind and the tide, since each ship had had not one but two anchors out against the strong currents of Calais Roads, and these anchors were still buried in the sea-bed; spares, if any, would have been stowed away and not immediately available to prevent the ships from being swept away into the night.

From the Spanish point of view the situation was

*The Duke of Medina Sidonia, Lord High Admiral of the Armada. Modern historians have sympathized with his plight as a non-sailor charged to carry out an impossible mission. This painting shows the Duke as an old man; there are no known portraits of him in 1588, when he was only thirty-seven.*

potentially disastrous: the Armada's battle order was broken at last. An English minister, Robert Cecil, wrote to his father that the Armada "would not have stirred from those roads" but for what he quaintly called "the device of the fireworks". And a Spaniard wrote bitterly that "The enemy were lucky. Their trick turned out exactly as they had planned: with eight ships they put us to flight, a thing they had not dared to attempt with a hundred and thirty."

At dawn, Medina Sidonia realized how things stood and sent out pinnaces to round up the strays as quickly as possible. When his pilots told him that it was dangerous to follow the fleet because of the shoals (shallows) along the coast, the Duke made the only honourable decision possible for a Spanish grandee: backed by the four warships accompanying the *San Martin*, he would buy time for the Armada to reassemble by standing out against the entire English fleet.

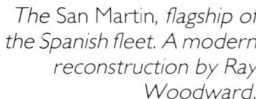

*The* San Martin, *flagship of the Spanish fleet. A modern reconstruction by Ray Woodward.*

# Diversion: the crippled giant

### The lure of loot

The English fleet remained in its anchorage overnight, waiting to see whether the fireships had done their work. Since there had been no additional fires or explosions, it must have seemed possible that they had passed harmlessly through the Armada. However, matters rarely seem so clear to the people involved in life-or-death events, and Admiral Sir William Wynter afterwards claimed that there had in fact been two direct hits. Night, nerves, imagination or poor eyesight led him to assert that "there were two great fires more than ours, and far greater and huger than any of our vessels that we fired could make".

He was quite wrong, although at the time there was no way for the English to prove or disprove his statement. But at daybreak it did become clear that the Spaniards had scattered and were highly vulnerable to an attack by the overwhelming mass of the English fleet. Every sailor must have known that the Lord High Admiral would send him into action straight away, before the Spaniards had a chance to re-form. At a signal from the *Ark*, trumpets blared and banners were raised. The entire fleet – about 140 vessels – weighed anchor and shook out its sails, ready to go into action.

It was about seven o'clock in the morning when Howard of Effingham gave the order to charge – "charge" was the word used, though nowadays it calls up mental pictures of cavalry rather than ships. Like the Elizabethan habit of referring to the fleets as "armies", it was a hangover from the grappling-and-boarding days, not long past, when battles at sea were decided by soldiers. Even the notion that ships and fleets should be commanded by sailors – rather than generals – was quite recent. Drake is usually credited with establishing the new practice; but when the supreme crisis occurred, neither Queen Elizabeth nor Philip II adhered to it fully, although their appointments were also influenced by non-military considerations of rank and precedence. Each fleet was commanded by an aristocrat, trained to arms (on land), with a more gifted navy man as his principal adviser. Medina Sidonia had Recalde; Howard's vice-admiral was Sir Francis Drake, a seaman famous throughout Europe and dreaded in

Don Alphonso Duke of
Medina, Cheife Comander
of ỹ Spanish Fleete.is·Iohn
Martin Recalde, a great Seaman.

In 1588 Sir Francis Drake was the most famous living seaman in Europe and the scourge of the Spanish Main. However, in the battles against the Armada he had to serve as second-in-command of the English fleet under the aristocratic Lord Howard.

*This curiosity is an English playing card carrying figures supposedly representing the Duke of Medina Sidonia and his second-in-command, Juan Martinez de Recalde. As in the English fleet, the aristocrat was placed in authority over the nation's greatest sailor. Recalde, aged sixty-two, made his last voyage with the Armada; he survived the hazards of the Irish coast and reached Spain, but died a few weeks later.*

all King Philip's ocean-bounded dominions as "El Draque", the scourge of Spanish America and the man who had "singed the King of Spain's beard" by his raid on Cadiz the year before.

Apart from his relatively humble birth, the only objection that might have been lodged against Drake as a fleet commander was that he understood more about buccaneering than about grand strategy. Though he was a rigid disciplinarian on his own ships, he had a carelessly individualistic attitude towards the concerted action needed in wartime. Only a few days earlier he had simply abandoned his post in order to capture a rich and helpless prize (the term for ships and other wartime booty that could be turned into cash by the captains and crews that took them). Drake's action infuriated another famous English seadog, Sir Martin Frobisher, who threatened that he would make Drake "spend the best blood in his belly". However, Frobisher was not expressing moral indignation: he just wanted a share of the loot. Most Englishmen were ardent patriots; but at sea,

**15**

patriotism and profit were almost always linked, and every sailor, from the great captains down to the humblest seaman, hoped to mend or make his fortune out of the spoils of war. Elizabethan ideas of wider responsibilities were still rudimentary; and on this Monday morning the fact was demonstrated by the Lord High Admiral himself.

### *The* San Lorenzo

Having ordered the fleet to go into action, Howard noticed a Spanish vessel, the *San Lorenzo*, crawling along close to the shore in an effort to reach Calais harbour. The *San Lorenzo* was the chief casualty of the Spaniards' hasty evacuation the night before: she had fouled her rudder on the chain of the *San Juan de Sicilia*, which had torn it off, and had then collided with another vessel. But although crippled, she could make some progress because she was not exclusively given over to sail: she was a galleass, part-galleon and part-galley. As well as sails, the *San Lorenzo* carried over three hundred convicts chained to her oars, and it was these "galley slaves" who were now pulling hard to reach the harbour. The Armada's four big galleasses had proved to be doughty fighters in earlier engagements; they were among the most heavily armed ships in the fleet, and they were potentially very dangerous in situations where their oars enabled them to make way while sailing ships lay becalmed. The *San Lorenzo*, the largest and most powerful of the galleasses, was also the flagship of the group, commanded by Don Hugo de Moncada; and it may have been these facts that determined Howard to finish her off, leaving Drake to lead the "charge". It was certainly his policy to weaken the Spaniards gradually, without taking too many risks: even when Monday's battle was done, he reported that "Their force is wonderful great and strong; and yet we pluck their feathers by little and little." The *San Lorenzo*, Howard might have argued, was one of the Armada's larger feathers. On the other hand, the galleass was hardly likely to be allowed out of the harbour again by the French (let alone repaired and sent out in time to locate the Armada); and, at least by later standards, there is something definitely amiss in the action of a commander-in-chief who diverts his entire squadron from the main engagement of the day. It still seems most likely that Howard – just like the buccaneering Drake – forgot all about grand strategy and succumbed to the lure of a rich and helpless prize.

If the Lord High Admiral believed that he could dispose of the *San Lorenzo* in short order, events proved him quite wrong. His squadron became embroiled in an action that lasted between three and six hours – different accounts give different estimates – and he therefore missed most of the decisive battle between the English fleet and the Armada! When Hugo de Moncada realized that Howard's ships were bearing down on him, he steered the *San Lorenzo* still closer to the shore – too close, as it turned out, for she soon ran aground in the surf. After this, the stranded galleass heeled over in the direction of the beach, leaving her guns on the seaward side pointing uselessly towards the sky. But the English guns were equally ineffective, since Howard's ships could not get within range of the *San Lorenzo* without themselves running aground. Galleons drew more water (that is, needed to be in a greater depth of water in order to stay afloat) than galleasses; and the beach at Calais sloped so gently that, even a long way out to sea, the water was dangerously shallow for a big sailing ship.

## A brisk fight

Perhaps this was the moment when Howard ought to have rejoined the fleet, leaving the *San Lorenzo* beached and probably permanently out of action. Instead, he sent sixty men in the *Ark*'s longboat to board the galleass. Other ships' boats joined in, filled with loot-hungry seamen. A small English ship, the *Margaret and John*, ventured too close and herself became stuck on a sandbank, but nonetheless sent out a pinnace with an enthusiastic contingent to fight the Spaniards.

Boarding the *San Lorenzo* proved to be a difficult assignment. Because she had heeled over towards dry land, her seaward rail stood up high above the surf, making a barricade that had to be laboriously climbed rather than quickly scrambled over by the attackers. It also provided excellent cover from which Spanish marksmen could fire down on to the Englishmen in their open boats. There were almost seven hundred men on the *San Lorenzo*, including 234 soldiers; and although some may have abandoned ship (including the 312 convict oarsmen, if they were given the chance), Moncada was left with a formidable force in a good defensive position. Richard Tomson, Lieutenant of the *Margaret and John*, described the situation in a letter written on the following day: "We continued a pretty skirmish with our small shot against theirs, they being ensconced within their ship and very high over us, we in our open pinnaces and far under them, having nothing to shroud and cover us." In the spirited exchanges of musket-fire between the two sides, the English began to suffer casualties and the lieutenant in charge of the *Ark*'s longboat, Amyas Preston, was "sore hurt". Then, quite suddenly, it was all over: a lucky shot hit Don Hugo de Moncada between the eyes, killing him instantly, and the Spaniards' discipline collapsed. Until this moment, the English had been far from certain of success. Like many men in the sixteenth century, Richard Tomson attributed the outcome to divine intervention: "It pleased God, by killing the captain with a musket shot, to give us victory above all hope or expectation; for the soldiers leaped overboard by heaps on the other side and fled with the shore, swimming and wading. Some escaped with being wet; some, and that very many, were drowned." The English boats closed in, and the Spanish officers, who had remained at their posts, held out two handkerchiefs on the points of rapiers, signifying their willingness to surrender. English seamen swarmed on to the *San Lorenzo*, took possession of her, and began to strip her bare; the prisoners, along with everything on board that could be moved, were transported back to Howard's ships.

Even this was not the end of the episode. During the fighting, crowds of people had gathered on the shore, taking advantage of French neutrality to watch the fight without danger to themselves. Once it was over, representatives of the governor of Calais, Monsieur Gourdan, appeared on board the *San Lorenzo* to remind the victors that not all the spoils were theirs: since they were in French waters, the ship itself, the rigging, and the guns belonged to Gourdan. It is not clear whether the English disputed the claim, or whether some of them simply ran amok in a buccaneering frenzy; at any rate, a number of English sailors scrambled ashore and began to hold up and rob the citizens who had come out to watch.

At this point the governor intervened forcefully. The guns of his fort started to bombard the English boats, which rapidly took off the remaining men and made their way back to Howard's squadron. This made a rather lame ending to an encounter that had been exciting and profitable, if not of much relevance to the great battle raging only a few kilometres away.

# The duke defiant

## *Early morning*

The naval engagement that Howard of Effingham almost missed is usually called the battle of Gravelines, after the village lying just above Calais. When the fighting started, the combatants were certainly close to Gravelines – perhaps ten or eleven kilometres out to sea – although they probably moved further away from it in the course of the day.

To the Spaniards and most other Europeans, the date of this decisive encounter was 8th August, 1588. They used the New Style or Gregorian calendar, issued in 1582 by Pope Gregory XIII. The Protestant English obstinately refused to accept this "popish" reform, and clung to the Old Style or Julian calendar, which had originated in a decree issued by Julius Caesar in 46 BC. As a result, all late sixteenth-century English datings were ten days earlier than their Spanish equivalents, and so in English eyes the battle of Gravelines took place on 29th July. The Gregorian system eventually won, although England held out until 1752 before adopting it, and it was only introduced in Russia after the 1917 Revolution! When writing about the past, it is still difficult to know which style of dating to use when the subject-matter involves more than one country; even the most modern histories of the Armada differ from one another and so give apparently inconsistent dates for the events they describe. This is a rich source of puzzlement and confusion that all students and pleasure-readers need to bear in mind. This book tries to avoid a too-English point of view, and therefore adopts the New Style dating, taking up the story on the morning of 8th August.

The English fleet moved in to attack the *San Martin*, flagship of the Duke of Medina Sidonia, which stood out ready to fight a holding action while the bulk of the Spanish fleet extricated itself from the coastal shallows. Within the following hour or so the Duke was to take on the most famous English seamen of the day – Drake, Hawkins and Frobisher. In the absence of Howard and his squadron, Sir Francis Drake led the charge in his galleon the *Revenge*. The English were determined to cripple the Armada before it could re-form, and therefore abandoned their policy of long-distance

bombardment, which had so far produced only limited results. They would go in close and deliver ship-smashing broadsides, relying for success on their superior speed, manoeuvrability and (perhaps) gunnery – and, arguably most important of all, on their effective superiority in numbers and force; since the Spaniards were scattered, the English squadrons could descend on individual vessels or small groups, surrounding them and sending in ship after ship to pulverize them.

## The Duke at bay

This was the fate of the *San Martin*. Like Drake, though for a different reason, Medina Sidonia held his fire until the last moment: the *San Martin* was already desperately short of heavy shot. At perhaps a hundred metres, the *Revenge*'s bow guns roared out; then Drake's vessel turned, and both combatants let fly with tremendous broadsides. The *Revenge* did not escape unscathed; some of the rigging collapsed as the ship was "pierced through by cannon-balls of all sizes, which were flying everywhere between the two fleets, and was riddled with every kind of shot".

By contrast, there is no way of knowing how much damage the *Revenge* inflicted, since this was only the first of many batterings received by the *San Martin*. The *Revenge* was followed closely by Thomas Fenner's *Nonpareil*, which may well have let off her broadside before the *San Martin* had had time to reload; and the other ships of Drake's squadron followed suit. Shortly afterwards Sir Martin Frobisher came up in the *Triumph*, and Sir John Hawkins also joined the attack in the *Victory*, backed by the *Mary Rose, Dreadnought* and *Swallow* from his squadron. By this time, however, the *San Marcos*, the *San Juan* and one or two other Spanish galleons had appeared and were striving to take some of the pressure off the *San Martin*, which had stood up to the English attacks amazingly well, although probably now leaking and holed both above and below her waterline.

Drake never returned to this fight, but headed away to the north-east. There is no record of what he did after this; the only important reference to his movements is a furious outburst by Frobisher, who accused Drake of outright desertion. "He came bragging up at the first indeed, and gave them his prow and his broadside; and then kept his luff [kept his distance] and was glad that he was gone again like a

◁ *Martin Frobisher, a tough, high-tempered Yorkshireman in his fifties, commanded one of the English squadrons against the Armada and was knighted during the campaign. His craft, the* Triumph, *was the biggest ship in the English fleet. This portrait is by Cornelius Kettle.*

At fifty-six, John Hawkins was the oldest of the English commanders who saw action against the Armada. Twenty years earlier, at San Juan de Ulua, the Spaniards had ambushed his ships while they were trading illicitly, an incident that set off the long unofficial war between English sailors and Spain. As treasurer and comptroller of the navy Hawkins was largely responsible for creating the royal galleons that did the greatest damage to the Armada.

cowardly knave or traitor – I rest doubtful, but the one I will swear. [I don't know which, but I'm ready to swear it was one or the other.]"

Frobisher's view was clearly a thoroughly prejudiced one: he had a terrible temper, and he was still angry about the way in which Drake had poached a Spanish prize a week earlier. Everything we know about Drake suggests that, if he acted on an impulse, it was one of ferocity rather than cowardice. There are more plausible explanations of his behaviour, the most common of which is that he intended to wreak havoc among the Spanish ships that Medina Sidonia was protecting, driving them on to the shoals before they could get clear and re-form. If so, Drake failed – perhaps because not enough English captains had the wit to divine his intentions and follow him. Martin Frobisher certainly thought of nothing else but taking or sinking the *San Martin*. Frobisher's

*Triumph* was the biggest ship in the English fleet, an 1100-ton giant with a five-hundred-man crew: it was fully capable of taking on the Spanish flagship, whose capture would certainly have ranked as the crowning feat of the day. But although the *Triumph* stood and fought her, and the rest of Frobisher's squadron passed to and fro pouring in shot, the *San Martin* did not sink. Despite leaks and splintered rigging, she remained in action, a remarkable testimony to the skill of the Spanish shipwrights.

### The crescent re-forms

Thanks to Medina Sidonia's heroic stand, his other fighting ships were gradually able to get away from the shoals and, helped by an ebb-tide, succeeded in joining him. Eventually there were enough of them to constitute a formidable-looking force, and by about nine o'clock in the morning, when Sir William Wynter arrived in the *Vanguard*, they had even managed to fall into a semblance of their characteristic V- or crescent-shaped line. It was this formation that the English had found it so hard to make an impression on during the earlier battles in the Channel, although then the Spanish supply ships and troop transports had lain snugly protected behind the line of warships. Now they were still strung out along the coast of Flanders, but the warships played essentially the same protective role, taking the brunt of the furious English attacks. According to Wynter's account, "They went into a proportion of a half moon . . . in their wings, their galleasses, armados of Portugal, and other good ships, in the whole to the number of sixteen in a wing, which did seem to be of their principal shipping." In other words, the Spaniards had somehow assembled and formed into line about thirty-two of their best fighting ships, in spite of everything the entire English fleet could do – a feat of nerve and seamanship that should not be underestimated merely because the English won the day. In fact it is one of the curious features of the entire campaign – a famous English victory which gave rise to the myth of a gallant little fleet defeating an overwhelmingly superior enemy – that the English generally did less than what was expected of them, while the supposedly landlubberly Spaniards often performed admirably. However, the English had better ships and, above all, more ammunition; and that decided the battle of Gravelines.

# The confusion of battle

## Free-for-all

It is not possible to give a strict hour-by-hour account of the long-drawn-out climax of the battle. We do not know exactly what was happening over the entire area, and neither did the men who took part; on the English side, they were not even certain of the result when it was all over. The age of fighting sail, which lasted into the nineteenth century, was still in its infancy, and it is unlikely that either side had any subtle or detailed plan of action; if they had, it was lost in the confusion of battle, amid the thunder of guns, the cries of the wounded, and the great clouds of gunsmoke swirling round the combatants. Any communication between ships could only have been a brief shouted message between neighbours – mostly defiance if they were enemies, and appeals or advice if they were fellow-countrymen. Each captain had to take his own decisions without consulting his superiors, and the battle of Gravelines has often been described as a free-for-all.

This did not mean it was every man for himself, with no co-operation between ships: the English vessels clustered in large numbers round likely prey, and other Spanish craft laboured valiantly to come to the rescue. And there does seem to have been a general pattern in the fleet movements, with the English manoeuvring to jostle the enemy closer and closer to the sandbanks off Dunkirk, while the Spaniards tried to edge away towards the north. As the course of the battle demonstrated, the Spaniards were still in a hopelessly inferior situation despite their achievement in re-forming: they were outnumbered, either badly mauled or exhausted by the struggle against the elements, and short of ammunition. The main English tactic was to surround any ship that was isolated or in trouble, and knock it to pieces at short range. The Spaniards certainly fought well and honourably, frequently taking great risks to aid one another; Medina Sidonia in the *San Martin* and Recalde in the *San Juan* set worthy examples, remaining in the hottest part of the battle despite severe punishment. But in this kind of action the English had tremendous advantages because of their speedier craft and handier seamanship: they were able to concentrate their forces far more quickly than the clumsier Spanish vessels could come to the rescue; and when this happened they could,

English and Spanish fleets in combat off Calais. The engraving, like that on page 6, was made in the eighteenth century from one of a set of tapestries commissioned by Howard of Effingham. The portraits in the frame are of the English captains.

if necessary, sheer off at speed and descend on a new victim elsewhere. In practice, however, the surrounded vessel seems usually to have been so crippled by the time relief arrived that the attackers were able to turn on the newcomer. And as the day wore on, there was probably less and less need for evasive action on the part of the English since the Spaniards used up all their heavy shot and were reduced to defending themselves with small-arms fire from arquebuses and muskets. This was not just a futile gesture: the English ships came in so close that their sailors were within range of Spanish handguns, which certainly inflicted some casualties. All the same, it is clear that the Armada's fighting ships were more or less helpless during the closing stages of the battle, reliant for their survival only on the stoutness of their hulls. The English captains were right to shorten their range: their guns did far more damage than in earlier battles. And yet by mid-afternoon they had seemingly still failed to deliver the ship-smashing blows they had hoped for. Some of the Spanish and Portuguese galleons looked like floating ruins, but not one had gone to the bottom.

### English accounts of the fight

Although we cannot trace the general sequence of events, we do know of certain vivid episodes. Surprisingly, fewer of these were recorded on the English side, and not all of them are entirely reliable. For example, Sir William Wynter wrote to Sir Francis Walsingham (the English minister of state most directly concerned) describing (inaccurately) the sending in of the fireships. He went on to describe how he came up at about nine o'clock and found the Spaniards back in formation. Then "My fortune was to make choice to charge their starboard wing without shooting of any ordnance [artillery] until we came within six score [paces?] of them; and some of our ships did follow me." Without other correspondents to enlighten him, Walsingham might well have supposed that it was Wynter who led the first charge in the battle, which had actually been in progress for about two hours when he arrived. According to Wynter, the Spanish ships on the starboard wing were so alarmed that they fled, in such haste that "four of them did entangle themselves one aboard the other. One of them recovered himself, and so shrouded [hid] himself among the fleet; the rest, how they were beaten I will leave it to the report of some of the

Spaniards that leapt into the seas and [were] taken up, and are now in the custody of some of our fleet." Wynter implies, though he does not directly assert, that he and his men sank three Spanish ships, which was certainly not true.

A more intimate view of the action comes from a narrative written by an Italian named Petruccio Ubaldino who lived in England. It was commissioned by Sir Francis Drake – a fact that, incidentally, illustrates the prestige of Italian writers in Renaissance Europe, since an ardent patriot such as Drake might have been expected to give preference to one of "God's Englishmen". Ubaldino offers a curious and authentic-sounding description of Drake's cabin which brings home the dangers and also the sheer duration of the fight, from which at least some of the participants took time out to rest: "His cabin was twice pierced by cannon-balls and there was an occasion on which two gentlemen, who towards evening had retired to rest a little, and one of them lying upon the bed, when it was broken under him by a saker [type of cannon] ball, without his taking the least hurt. And shortly afterwards the Earl of Northumberland, who had come to fight as a volunteer, and Sir Charles Blount, were resting on the same bed in the same place when it was again hit by a ball from a demi-culverin [another type of cannon] which passed through the cabin from one side to another without doing any harm than scrape the foot, taking off the toes of one who was there with them." Presumably these were the toes of a servant or some other commoner, since Ubaldino did not think him worth naming.

### Spanish eye-witness

Spanish accounts of the Armada's campaign are fuller, and sometimes more exciting. The Duke of Medina Sidonia kept a diary and wrote a complete account of the expedition for Philip II, but his stiff-upper-lip attitude and unwillingness to blame anyone makes his tale rather flat. By contrast, Pedro Coco Calderon, chief purser on the *San Salvador*, wrote a diary that gives us a rare glimpse of the battle at what was probably its hottest point.

The ship in deepest trouble was the Portuguese galleon *San Felipe*, which probably lay on the starboard wing attacked by Sir William Wynter's squadron. Lord Henry Seymour's ships also joined in, and according to Calderon the *San Felipe* found herself "surrounded by seventeen of the enemy's ships, which directed heavy fire against her on both sides and on her stern. The enemy approached so close that the muskets and arquebuses of the galleon were brought into service, killing a large number of men on the enemy ships. They [the English] did not dare, however, to come to close quarters [to grapple and board], but kept up a hot artillery fire from a distance, disabling the rudder, breaking the foremast, and killing over two hundred men in the galleon." One of Calderon's remarks – that the English "did not dare" to board – reflects the Spaniards' feeling that every encounter at sea should culminate in a hand-to-hand fight between soldiers, and that the English were not being entirely honourable in trying to decide the battle by purely naval means! This feeling was probably intensified by the Spaniards' frustration as they fought on in a near-helpless condition.

The *San Mateo* came to the aid of the *San Felipe*, a brave – possibly rash – decision if there were really seventeen English vessels pounding the Portuguese galleon. The *San Mateo* was soon in trouble too: "Some of the enemy's ships attacked . . . and inflicted much damage. One of the enemy's ships came alongside the galleon and an Englishman jumped on board; but our men cut him to pieces at once" – an example, presumably, of a man going quite crazy with battle-fever. Then the Armada's flagship, the *San Martin*, came up, accompanied by the *San Salvador*, the ship on which Calderon was serving. The *San Salvador* became involved in a fierce fight with two big English ships, and no doubt Calderon was kept too busy to notice what was going on elsewhere. At any rate he concentrates on the misfortunes of his own vessel, "her bows, side, and half her poop being exposed for four hours to the enemy's fire, during which she had a large number of men killed and wounded, and her hull, sails and rigging were much damaged. She leaked greatly through shot holes, and finally the *Rata Encoronada*, under Don Alonso de Levya, came to her assistance, distinguishing herself greatly. On board the *Rata* there fell Don Pedro de Mendoza and other persons. They had to defend themselves against three flagships, a vice-flagship and ten or twelve other war vessels."

And so it went on, with one Spanish ship after another taking savage punishment. Towards the end, the *San Felipe* was in a terrible state, with her upper deck destroyed, her rigging in shreds, both her pumps broken, and five of her starboard guns knocked out of action. Instead of surrendering, her commander, Don Francisco de Toledo, ordered the grappling hooks to be made ready and challenged the enemy to board the *San Felipe*, vainly hoping to get to grips with the Englishmen at last. At least one of his enemies was impressed, or perhaps hoped to bluff the Spaniards to surrender: an Englishman, "standing in the maintop with his sword and buckler, called out 'Good soldiers that you are, surrender on the fair terms we offer.' But the only answer he received was a gunshot which brought him down in sight of everyone." The Spaniards prepared to fight on with muskets and arquebuses, but it was the English who withdrew: perhaps they had exhausted their ammunition. There was of course no point in taking unnecessary risks by attempting to board the *San Felipe*, but – understandably – the Spaniards jeered at the retreating vessel, calling the English cowards and "Protestant hens" (an early version of the slang term "chicken" = cowardly).

### End of a battle

The fight seems to have gone on until some time between four and six o'clock in the afternoon. It was ended by a sudden squall – harsh gusts of wind and a blinding downpour of rain – which caused both sides to break off while they shortened sail and struggled against the elements. When the weather cleared, the Spaniards were further north, out of immediate danger of the sandbanks and defiantly re-forming in readiness to fight on. But by now the English ships were no better supplied than the Spaniards', and so "when every man was weary with labour, and our cartridges spent and munitions wasted [used up] . . . we ceased" (Wynter). The day's fighting was done and, although neither side knew it, the battle was over.

Unlike their enemies, the English were able to replenish their supplies, and Howard at once sent off a note to Sir Francis Walsingham asking for powder, shot and victuals – and including a sharp rebuke for Walsingham's bureaucratic efforts to make him state just how much ammunition was needed, "which, by reason of the uncertainty of the service, no man can do; therefore I pray you to send with all speed as much as you can." Until it arrived, the English fleet could do no more than shadow the Armada.

The Spaniards did not know this, and must have been close to despair. Although the Armada had apparently survived intact, many of the ships were in a pitiable condition, leaking, with shattered decks, riggings in shreds, and gunports caked with the blood of the 600 dead and 800 wounded men. Their exhausted crews, nourished by mouldy biscuits and foul water, had to conduct perfunctory mass sea-burials and patch their vessels as best they could. The situation was all the worse because the heavy seas made it impossible to carry out major repairs; the *San Martin* herself, badly holed, was only kept afloat by strenuous pumping. And, as darkness approached, there was the ever-present danger of the shoals to a fleet that dare not anchor (perhaps could not after the cable-cutting of the night before) for fear of fireships.

The after-effects of the battle began to be felt at about seven o'clock in the evening. The much battered *San Felipe*, in which sixty men had already been killed and two hundred others wounded, fired several shots to indicate that she was in dire straits. A hulk, the *Donicella*, reached her and took off the survivors; but then an alarm was raised that the hulk too was sinking. Don Francisco de Toledo declared that if that was the case he would rather be drowned in a galleon than a hulk, and he and his second-in-command jumped back into the *San Felipe*. This splendid gesture turned into black comedy when it transpired that the hulk was not in fact going down, while the helpless *San Felipe* began to drift away with the two impetuous Spaniards on board. The captain of the *San Mateo*, Don Diego Pimental, showed a similarly misplaced gallantry, refusing to abandon ship. During the night his ship also drifted away, and both vessels eventually fetched up on the Flanders coast, where they fell into the hands of enemies, the Dutch rebels against Philip II who were in league with the English.

More disheartening, because it happened in the sight of the entire fleet, was the fate of the *Maria Juan*, one of the galleons in Recalde's squadron. Her signal for help was answered by the *San Martin*, which got close enough to send boats to the rescue; but the stricken vessel foundered very quickly. Only one boat-load of survivors – men who had managed to cling on to the spars and rigging until the last moment – was taken off in time. About two hundred and fifty men, including the dead and wounded, went down with the *Maria Juan*.

In spite of seas, wind and shoals, the rest of the fleet survived the night. When dawn broke on Tuesday, 9th August, with the victorious English fleet apparently ready to finish the business of the day before, most of the Spaniards on shipboard must have believed that the end of the Armada was at hand.

# Aftermath: the Armada in flight

### The miraculous wind

Early on Tuesday morning, the *San Martin* and the other first-class Spanish ships took up their positions in the rear of the Armada, still ready to ward off their pursuers if they could. But it soon became clear that the Spaniards were threatened by an enemy even more lethal than the English. During the night they had maintained a course roughly parallel with the Flemish (modern Belgian) coast, but now a strong wind was blowing them towards the Zealand shoals, on which they would surely run aground and be pounded to pieces by the surf. Trapped between the elements and the English, Medina Sidonia decided that it was preferable to die fighting. He ordered the fleet to rally to the rearguard, and offered battle.

The English fleet refused the challenge. The reason was almost certainly that they lacked sufficient ammunition to sustain a full-scale engagement. There was, in fact, an element of bluff in their shadowing of the Spaniards; neither side seems to have realized that the other was in no condition to carry on the fight. At the time, the Spaniards assumed that the English were simply standing off to see the Armada destroyed without their having to take any risks; for the Spanish ships were losing their fight with the wind and currents. Their anchors failed to stick in the sandy sea-bed, and they were slowly and inexorably driven towards the sands.

The captain of the *San Martin* later described the drama that followed – how the Duke refused all suggestions of surrender, putting his trust in God, and how the leadsman (whose job was to measure the depth of the water, using a lead-weighted line) called first seven fathoms, then six, then only five. Just when the Spaniards must have been steeling themselves against an impact that seemed bound to come within moments, the wind changed abruptly and the Armada was blown into the safety of the open sea. This was an age when most men thought of the winds as directly controlled by God and expressing his will; but the Spaniards naturally regarded the last-moment salvation of their fleet as a miracle of miracles.

### Flight and pursuit

That night Medina Sidonia held a council of war. The Spanish ships were battered and leaking; there were already hundreds of wounded or sick on board; every captain was demanding ammunition which the Duke could not supply; and food was running out fast. Nevertheless the council decided to do battle again, or else to seize one of the English ports – if the wind changed. No one can say whether this decision was made out of desperation, a sense of duty, or bravado, since the wind did not change: it drove the Armada northwards, away from the Channel ports and away from Parma. In that case, the council had decided, the Armada would sail right round the British Isles and return to Spain (see the map on page 36). It was bound to be a hazardous voyage, through badly charted waters that were quite unknown to the Spaniards; but there was probably no alternative that was both realistic and honourable.

The English were of course ignorant of their enemies' intentions; they resolved to shadow the Armada, ready to prevent it doubling back and also to intervene if the Spaniards attempted a military strike in the Firth of Forth against neutral but Protestant Scotland. The English council of war embodied this decision in a ringing declaration, signed by all the captains present and conveyed to the Privy Council (in effect, the English government), which ended with a sharp comment on the inadequacies of the supply system:

> "We whose names are hereunder written have determined and agreed in council to follow and pursue the Spanish fleet until we have cleared our own coast and brought the Frith [the Firth of Forth] west of us; and then to return back again, as well to re-victual our ships, which stand in extreme scarcity, as also to guard and defend our own coast at home; with further protestation that, if our wants of victuals and munition were supplied, we would pursue them to the furthest that they durst have gone. C. Howard. T. Howard. Fra. Drake. John Hawkyns. Thomas Fenner. George Coumbreland. Edmonde Sheffeylde. Edw. Hoby."

The English captains acted as they had declared they would, turning back in about the latitude of Newcastle when it became plain that the Armada had no designs on the Firth of Forth. But, even now, two pinnaces were detailed to follow

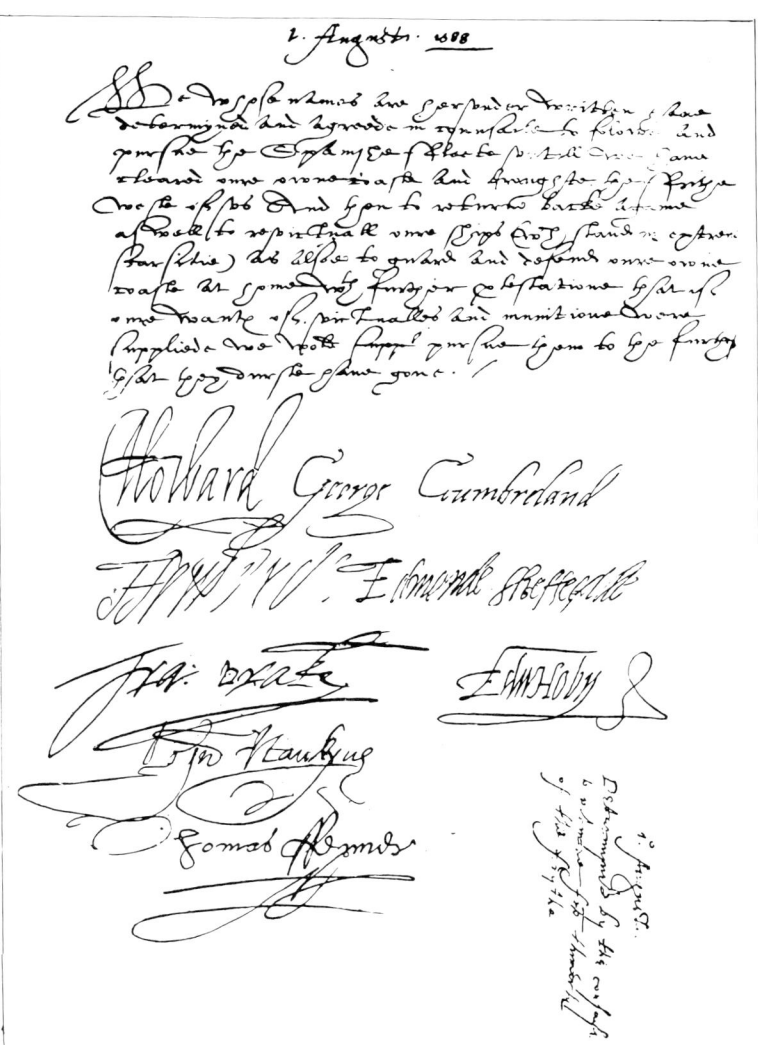

*The declaration signed by the English commanders stating their resolution to pursue the Spaniards.*

the Spaniards and report on their movements, just in case they did something unexpected. The Spaniards were of course in no condition to go in for elaborate stratagems, but the English did not know that. The English fleet had accomplished its most important task – it had prevented the junction between the Armada and Parma's invasion force – and it had given the Spaniards a drubbing. But the Spanish fleet was still intact and apparently dangerous. It was on the night *after* the battle of Gravelines that Howard wrote to Sir Francis Walsingham describing the Armada as "wonderfully great and strong"; evidently he, like the other English captains, expected further battles. Because they had sent so few of the enemy ships to the bottom, the English at first failed to realize the completeness of their victory. In his letter to Walsingham, Howard gave slightly more space to his exploit in taking the galleass *San Lorenzo* than to the entire battle of Gravelines; and even Sir Francis Drake, though declaring that "this day's service hath much appalled the enemy", mainly dwelt on the fact that "God hath given us so good a day in forcing the enemy so far to leeward as I hope in God the Prince of Parma and the Duke of Sidonia shall not shake hands this few days". Nothing written by the English captains in the first few days after the battle would have led anyone to suppose that it had been a decisive engagement; and their tone only began to change as it became clear that the Armada was in flight.

*Queen Elizabeth at Tilbury, where she made a famous speech to her army in August 1588. By this time the decisive battle of Gravelines had already been fought, and the Armada was in flight. But it was not at first clear that the danger was over, and Englishmen remained ready to put up a desperate defence against the anticipated invasion. The painting is on a panel at St Faith's Church, Gaywood, near King's Lynn, Norfolk.*

*According to tradition, the Armada jewel was given by Queen Elizabeth to her Vice-Chamberlain, after the defeat of the Armada. Inside is a miniature of the Queen. On the front, with appropriate nautical imagery, England is represented as an ark* tranquilla per unda saevas, *"tranquil amid the raging waters". The jewel is 7 cm high, made of enamelled gold set with diamonds and rubies.*

The authorities were even slower to rejoice: when Howard returned, he was met with a note from the Queen asking what treasures had been taken and why he had not boarded the Spanish ships; she was still thinking in terms of the past – of profitable English buccaneering expeditions to the Spanish Main – and evidently had no appreciation of the naval tactics that had defeated the Armada. She was also running out of money; and since it was at least clear that the immediate danger was past, she ordered that most of the fleet should be disbanded. Soon the ports of south-east England were filled with discharged sailors begging in the streets and dying in the open like flies from the diseases bred by shipboard conditions.

Only on 18th August was a thanksgiving service held at St Paul's Cathedral. Even then, there were fears that the Armada, with thousands of soldiers on board, might descend on Ireland. Finally, in November, the Queen, the Court and the City Livery Companies went in solemn procession to give thanks at the Cathedral. Medals were struck, verses composed, and the defeat of the Armada entered English history and myth. But by that time it had become clear that the Spaniards had met with utter ruin.

*One of the medals issued to commemorate the defeat of the Armada. This was the first historical event for which medals were struck by an English sovereign.*

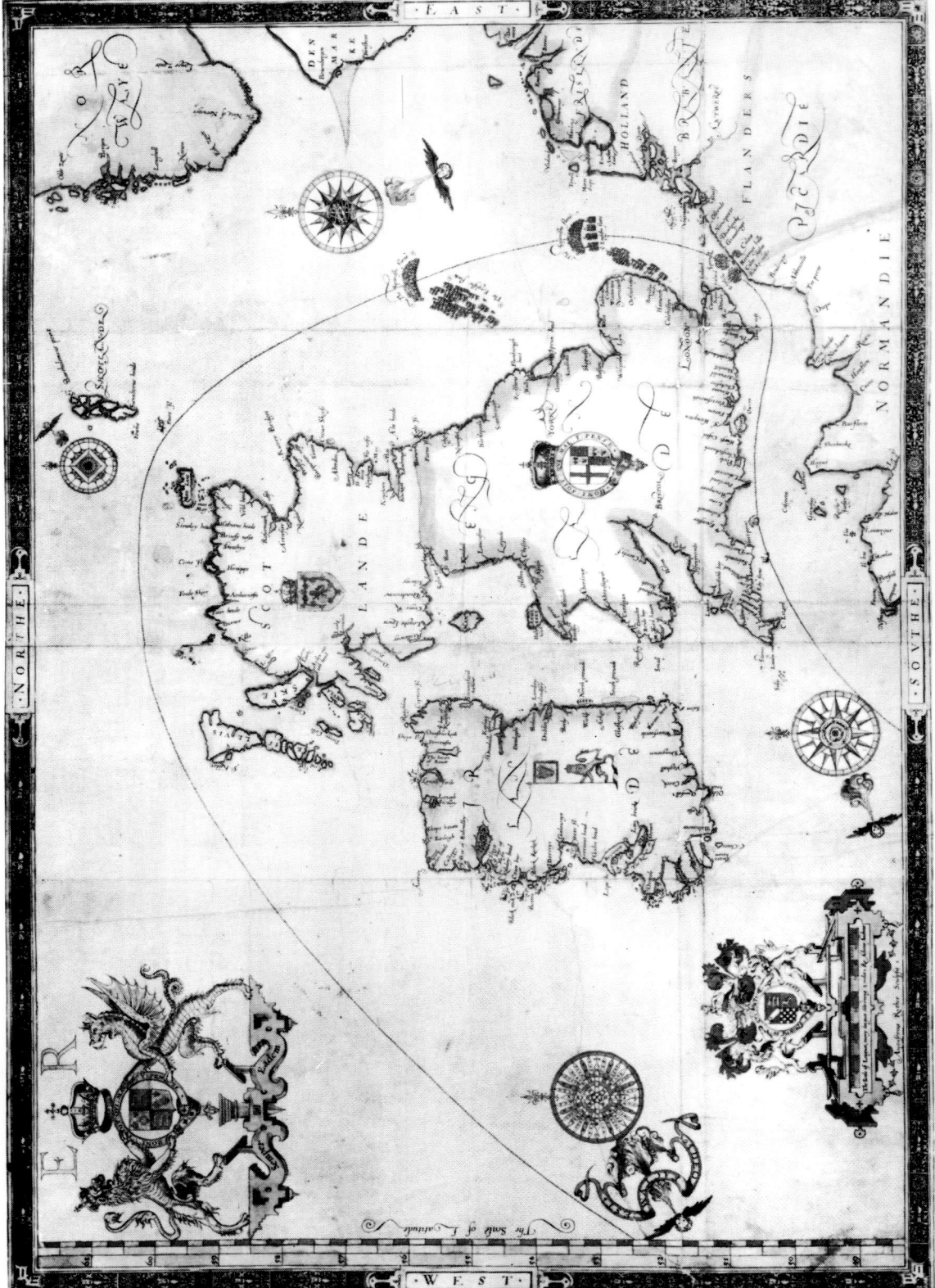

*A triumphal portrait of Howard of Effingham. In the background are depictions of his two greatest successes; (left) the defeat of the Armada and (right) the English raid on Cadiz of 1596.*

## A calamitous voyage

For ten days after the "miracle" of the wind, the Spanish ships managed to stay together; they ran before the wind into the North Sea and then, taking advantage of a change in wind direction, passed between the Orkney and Shetland Islands into the Atlantic. Both ships and men were in poor condition, and food was strictly rationed: each man had only eight ounces of hard tack (biscuit), a pint of water and half a pint of wine to last an entire day. In spite of this, the Duke of Medina Sidonia planned to take the Armada out into the Atlantic, avoiding the dangerous west coast of Ireland, and sail directly for the northern ports of Spain. As subsequent events showed, the plan was a feasible one; and if the fleet had stayed

◁ *Contemporary map showing the Armada's route along the Channel, through the North Sea and round the British Isles. Despite the course indicated, many Spanish ships in fact failed to clear the west of Ireland and were wrecked on its rocky coastline.*

37

together it might have worked. But the Atlantic gales were too much for it, and somewhere beyond Cape Wrath (the north-westernmost corner of Scotland) the Armada was scattered and never again re-formed.

From this point the voyage became increasingly nightmarish. The huge seas and rough weather of the North Atlantic were a terrible ordeal for the diminished and enfeebled crews of damaged ships; more and more men fell sick, thanks to lack of nourishment, foul drinking water and the generally insanitary conditions of shipboard life. (Things were not much different on English ships, and at this very time English sailors were succumbing on shore to infections caught during the campaign against the Armada.) All things considered, the Spanish galleons stood up to the Atlantic very well; but many of the merchantmen and other ships – designed for use in calmer Mediterranean waters – failed to survive. Most of the Spanish vessels probably became hopelessly lost. Some foundered and sank without trace; many more turned up on the west coast of Ireland, whether inadvertently or because they were desperate for food and water. And it was there that the worst disasters occurred.

This was a dangerous coast at all times, but the Spanish ships must have been especially vulnerable because they had lost their massive principal anchors on the night of the fireships; any remaining anchors they possessed would not have withstood the ferocity of the Atlantic winds and waves. Most of them were unable to avoid being driven ashore on to the sands, where they were soon broken up by the surf; some crews were even unluckier, and perished immediately as their vessel was flung on to the rocks. Over the years, divers have identified no fewer than twenty-six Spanish wrecks on the Irish coast, proving that this was the most disastrous episode in the history of the Armada.

Many Spaniards failed to reach the shore alive; while those who managed to do so met with a horrible reception. For a long time, English propaganda insisted that the native Irish massacred the shipwrecked men; but this was a distortion of the truth. The Irish were certainly responsible for many deaths: when the exhausted Spaniards were flung on to the shore, they were set upon, stripped to the skin and robbed of any gold or jewels they had managed to bring away with them; and on occasion they were brutally murdered. The Irish were miserably poor and primitive – the Spaniards habitually referred to them as "savages" – and everything the newcomers possessed, down to their boots, was by comparison precious. But in a rough way the natives could be kind, recognizing the Spaniards as fellow-Catholics and allies against the hated English; and Irish chieftains even employed Spaniards as soldiers – a striking comment on the quality of men who might well have been broken by their sufferings.

By contrast, the English proved to be implacable enemies, bent on exterminating every Spaniard found in Ireland. This policy was initially understandable. The Lord Deputy, Sir William Fitzwilliam, had fewer than 2,000 men with whom to hold down a turbulent people who refused to accept English rule, culture or religion; and he assumed that the mighty Armada – or some other Spanish force – had landed with an army of conquest. However, when it became clear that the Spaniards were not invaders but wave-battered, half-starved castaways, the order to exterminate was not countermanded. Everywhere they were hunted down and interrogated; then every one – including every little cabin-boy – was taken out and hanged; the only exceptions were a small number of men whom the English believed to be rich and worth holding to ransom. A few hundred Spaniards did manage to hide out and were ferried to Scotland, though most of them were later killed when they were shipped to the Spanish Netherlands and were ambushed at sea by Dutch rebels. A handful may have escaped the English and settled in Ireland – though it is doubtful whether their presence can have darkened the complexions of people from the west of Ireland, as legend has always insisted.

From late September 1588, Spanish ships began to get home. Medina Sidonia had followed his own instructions, and arrived sick but safe; Recalde had ventured on to the Irish coast and got away again, though he died four days after entering port. Vessels continued to crawl in until mid-October; then, gradually, hopes that there would be new arrivals gradually faded. The scale of the disaster – almost half the fleet lost – became apparent. The King, who had listened impassively to increasingly gloomy reports, ordered that prayers for victory – offered in every church in Spain – should now cease.

# THE
# INVESTIGATION

## Why were England and Spain at war?

*The Anglo-Spanish alliance*

For the first half of the sixteenth century, England and Spain seemed to be natural allies. Spain had only emerged as a nation towards the end of the previous century, after the rulers of its two largest regions, Ferdinand of Aragon and Isabella of Castille, were married. The new power soon (1489) signed a treaty with the Tudor King of England, Henry VII, and in 1501 the ties between the two countries were strengthened by the marriage of Henry's eldest son, Prince Arthur, to the Spanish princess Catherine of Aragon. This was considered so important on both sides that, when Arthur died, the alliance was maintained by betrothing the widowed Catherine to Arthur's brother, who succeeded as Henry VIII in 1509, a few weeks before the marriage ceremony was performed.

*The logic of power*

The alliance made good power-political sense. France was the traditional enemy of England, and therefore the traditional ally of England's other main antagonist, the Scots, whom the English had for centuries tried (and failed) to subdue. It was natural for England to oppose the Franco-Scottish "auld alliance" by combining with one or more of France's neighbours. This had earlier meant Flanders (the Duchy of Burgundy) or the Holy Roman Emperor, whose authority nominally extended over most of central Europe; but in the sixteenth century it meant the steadily rising power of Spain.

*Politics and religion*

Early in the century, international politics were transformed by two major developments. One was an exceptional concentration of power in the hands of the Habsburg family, whose leading member was the Holy Roman Emperor Charles V – who was also King of Spain, Duke of Burgundy, Archduke of Austria, the ruler of much of Italy, and the lord of vast areas of newly-conquered Central and South America. The other was the Protestant Reformation initiated in 1517 by Martin Luther; as a result, Protestants and Catholics engaged for generations in ferocious conflicts, and the intermingling of power-politics and ideology infinitely complicated war and diplomacy in Europe.

**The alliance strained**

During the early years of his reign, Henry VIII followed the established policy, generally siding with Ferdinand of Spain, and later with the Emperor Charles V, against the French. Then a domestic crisis disrupted the alliance. Henry, desperate for an heir, divorced Catherine of Aragon and took Anne Boleyn as his wife. Since the Pope refused to permit the divorce, Henry threw off his authority and had himself declared supreme head of the Church in England; so that, if not exactly Protestant, England ceased to be a Roman Catholic country. The discarded and humiliated Catherine was Charles V's aunt, and furthermore Charles was a loyal son of the Church, like all the Habsburgs. The Tudor-Habsburg alliance was broken, and for a time it even seemed that the two great Catholic monarchs, Charles V and Francis I of France, might launch a joint attack on heretical England. But political considerations soon became uppermost once more, and in his last years Henry again waged war on France in alliance with Charles V.

**Alliance triumphant?**

During the brief reign of Edward VI (1547-53), the boy king's advisers established a thorough-going Protestant regime. But corruption, inflation and enclosures discredited their "reformed religion", and when Edward died his Catholic sister Mary had no difficulty in asserting her right to the throne and restoring the "old religion". Paradoxically, her reign (1553-58) saw the rehabilitation of Protestantism, since "Bloody Mary" burned – and so made martyrs of – some three hundred men and women who adhered to the new faith. She also embraced the Spanish alliance all too enthusiastically: despite the misgivings of her English advisers, she insisted on marrying Charles V's son Philip, soon to be King Philip II of Spain. The English were already notorious for their dislike of foreigners, and the prospect of subordinating English to Spanish interests was enough to set off a revolt. Wyatt's rebellion was suppressed and the marriage took place, although Philip and his entourage received an unmistakably chilly welcome. The worst English fears were not realized, since Philip did not become King of England but only Mary's consort, with no real say in English affairs; to Mary's sorrow, he in fact spent very little time in the country once it became clear that she could not give him an heir. All the same, she acted as a dutiful wife and led an ill-prepared England into yet another European war on the Habsburg side. The only result was the loss of Calais, an English possession of symbolic as well as economic value, since it was the last remaining fragment of the wide French dominions that Englishmen had once ruled in the stirring days of King Henry V.

**Enter Elizabeth** The Spanish alliance was no longer popular, and the accession of Queen Elizabeth I (1558-1603) made its continuation even more unlikely. As the daughter of Anne Boleyn, she was illegitimate in Catholic eyes, and therefore committed willy-nilly to the Protestant cause. But she was also cautious and highly practical by nature, and the religious settlement at the beginning of her reign was as moderate and conciliatory as she could persuade Parliament to make it. Even so, it was unmistakably Protestant, and might have been expected to alienate the deeply pious Philip II. But both he and the Queen had excellent reasons for remaining on good terms. Elizabeth had no wish to quarrel with the most powerful ruler in Europe (Philip had inherited all his father's dominions except the imperial title and the Austrian lands, which were arguably a liability rather than an asset); and the Low Countries, or Netherlands, which Philip ruled as Duke of Burgundy, constituted the main market for England's principal exports, wool and cloth. As for Philip, he had enough enemies without adding to them; and although Elizabeth was a heretic, the Catholic claimant to the English throne was from his point of view politically impossible. She was Mary, Queen of Scots, widow of the French king Francis II; if she replaced Elizabeth on the English throne, the entire British Isles would pass into the French camp. This was such an important consideration that Philip even proposed to Elizabeth; and despite her politely evasive answer, he protected her by using his influence with the Pope to put off her official excommunication as a heretic.

**Mary, Queen of Scots** Anglo-Spanish relations remained cordial for a decade, until two quite separate crises broke during 1568. One was caused by Mary, Queen of Scots, whose erratic career in Scotland ended with her utter defeat by the Protestant party and her flight into England. This was advantageous to the English in one respect: Scotland became a friendly fellow-Protestant

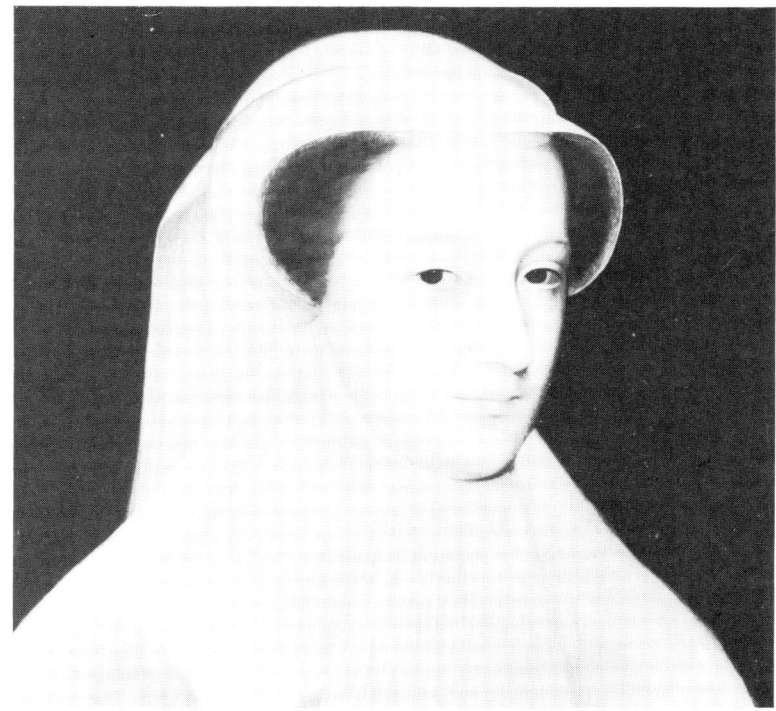

*Mary, Queen of Scots, as a young woman; the painting is by François Clouet. Mary's situation as a prisoner in England greatly complicated politics, both national and international.*

country. But Mary's presence in England made her a focus for Catholic plotting against Elizabeth. Until this time the Catholics had remained quiet, but in 1569 the Revolt of the Northern Earls in the name of the Old Religion gave the government cause for concern. Since Elizabeth jibbed at handing over a fellow-queen to rebels, but was equally reluctant to help a Catholic queen against fellow-Protestants, she felt she had no alternative but to keep Mary honourably confined in England, despite the attendant dangers.

**Helping the Dutch**    The other crisis arose from the Dutch Revolt against Philip II. As Duke of Burgundy, Philip ruled over a patchwork of wealthy provinces which had always largely run their own affairs. His efforts to introduce a centralized government and turn the Low Countries into a Spanish province caused a revolt which the Spaniards tried to suppress by harsh and energetic use of their army. Elizabeth had no wish to deprive Philip of his dukedom, but she was bound to oppose the creation of a powerful Spanish state in the Low Countries, only a few miles from the English coast. By this time, too, it had become clear that the old enemy, France, was much weakened by Catholic-Protestant conflicts, and that the most likely threat to English security – and the Protestant cause in general – came from the large Spanish empire. For these reasons Queen Elizabeth covertly helped the Dutch rebels, and in December 1568 risked taking openly hostile action against Spain. When bad weather forced some Spanish ships into English ports, the Queen ordered the confiscation of their cargoes of silver. This action fell just short of robbery, since King Philip had borrowed the money from Venetian lenders, and Elizabeth subsequently "persuaded" the Venetians to transfer the loan to her. But since the money was desperately needed to pay the Spanish troops in the Netherlands, Elizabeth had effectively intervened on the side of Philip's enemies.

***War avoided***

Each side proceeded to seize any "enemy" ship that lay in its ports, and a series of embargoes crippled Anglo-Spanish trade. But the conflict remained a "cold" war, without fighting, despite the tensions of the years that followed. In 1570 Pope Pius V issued a bull of excommunication, encouraging Catholics to assassinate the heretic Elizabeth, and in 1571 the Ridolfi plot against the Queen involved the Spanish ambassador in London. In response, Elizabeth negotiated an alliance with France in April 1572; it was felt to be such a political necessity that it even survived the Massacre of St Bartholomew a few months later, in which thousands of Huguenots (French Protestants) were murdered. However, the political situation in France was so unpredictable that French friendship was of limited value. On his side, Philip was

*A contemporary drawing of the Massacre of St Bartholomew in 1572. At four o'clock in the morning of 24th August – St Bartholomew's Day – the tocsin sounded in Paris and a general massacre of Protestants began. This was only one particularly sanguinary example of sixteenth-century religious intolerance. Others include the hanging, drawing and quartering of Jesuit missionaries in England, and the torturing and burning of English seamen by the Spanish Inquisition.*

still not convinced that it was in his interest to unseat Elizabeth or drive her into the arms of the French. So relations between the Catholic King and the Protestant Queen were quietly patched up.

***Undeclared war at sea***

A continuing source of friction between Spain and England was the semi-piratical behaviour of English seamen. The vast Spanish empire in the Americas, stretching from Florida to Tierra del Fuego, was officially closed to foreign trade. In practice, Spain could not supply all the wants of the Spanish settlers across the Atlantic, who welcomed English ships carrying a particularly valuable cargo – African slaves to work in their mines and fields. Spanish efforts to stop this illicit trade culminated in 1568, when a group of English ships led by John Hawkins was attacked – treacherously, as the English saw it – while they were refitting in the port of San Juan de Ulua. Only two ships, carrying Hawkins and the young Francis Drake, managed to get away.

After this, English seamen conducted their own private crusade against the Spaniards, who retaliated by either burning as a heretic or sending to the galleys any sailor who fell into their hands. The leading figure on the English side was Drake, whose exploits included carrying off a mule-train laden with a year's silver output on its journey from Peru to Nombre de Dios, the port from which such treasures were shipped to Spain. The incredibly rich silver mines of the Americas were vital in financing King Philip's many commitments (despite his vast empire, he was never far from bankruptcy), and English piracy was all the more galling because it was carried out with the Queen's complicity. The English expeditions were financed in a business-like way, with a number of investors taking up shares in the venture; and Elizabeth was perfectly willing to become one of them. She made the then huge profit of £160,000 – equivalent to six months' royal revenue – from the most spectacular of Drake's feats, his three-year trip round the world (1577-80), during which he raided the Spaniards' Pacific ports (underprotected because never before threatened) and captured the great Spanish treasure-ship *Cacafuego*. The Queen rewarded Drake – in Spanish eyes "the Master Thief of the Unknown World" – by knighting him on board his ship, the *Golden Hind*.

***The approaching crisis***

The undeclared war at sea was, among other things, a religious war; and in the 1580s European conflicts took on an

*Philip II's empire in 1580.*

increasingly ideological cast. By this time Philip had come to see himself as the chosen sword of Catholicism, since Catholic and Spanish interests seemed to have become identical. Philip's troops were still fighting in the Netherlands, where the revolt had taken on a largely Protestant character, and they had also become deeply involved on the Catholic side in the French wars of religion. The English queen was helping both the Dutch rebels and the Huguenots in France, and her seamen were preying on the Spaniards' oceanic lifelines: it was inevitable that Philip should begin to think of attacking a country that seemed to be the lynch-pin of international Protestantism – and especially once he had become king of Portugal (1580), adding a great colonial empire and a splendid fleet to his existing possessions.

In England, tempers were also rising as Catholicism came to be seen as internally subversive as well as an external danger. In the 1570s English priests, trained abroad at Douai and other seminaries, returned secretly from exile and prevented their flocks from compromising with Anglicanism; and in the 1580s they were followed by the intellectually even better-equipped Jesuits, whom Protestants specially hated and feared. In 1579 the Pope recruited Italian and Spanish volunteers and launched an invasion of Protestant England's weakest point – predominantly Catholic and ever-rebellious Ireland, which England held down by exploiting the divisions among the Irish and, when that failed, by brute force. The invasion, and the Irish risings that accompanied it, were defeated with difficulty. In England itself, Catholicism now became identified with treason; the anti-Catholic laws were made harsher, and captured priests and Jesuits were tortured and hanged, drawn and quartered as enemies of the state. Meanwhile plots centring on Mary, Queen of Scots, continued to be devised and discovered. Elizabeth's councils and parliaments – filled with men whose heads would roll if the Queen died and was succeeded by Mary – pressed for the prisoner's trial and execution. But Elizabeth was reluctant to shed the blood of a fellow-sovereign, or to provoke Catholic Europe more than was absolutely necessary; and for years she delayed taking this and other political initiatives.

**War**   Events forced her hand. In July 1584 the able Dutch leader, William the Silent, was assassinated. This was a critical

*William the Silent, leader of the Dutch Revolt. His assassination in 1585 prompted Queen Elizabeth to intervene in the Netherlands, an action that caused the final break between England and Spain.*

moment in the revolt, since the Spaniards were making spectacular progress under their great general Alexander Farnese, soon to become Duke of Parma: Bruges and Ghent fell to the Spaniards in 1584, and Brussels and Antwerp in 1585. At this point Elizabeth felt she must intervene openly, and she signed a treaty with the Dutch committing 6,000 men under the Earl of Leicester to the struggle against Spain. Although she insisted that she wished only to safeguard the Netherlands' ancient privileges, a compromise peace was no longer a likely outcome of the revolt, since the rebels had already declared that they aimed for nothing less than complete independence. So English actions now threatened Philip's empire and challenged his authority by land as well as by sea. There was never an official declaration, but it was clear that England and Spain were now at war.

The Earl of Leicester in his prime. There is little doubt that as a young woman Elizabeth was in love with this magnificent courtier, and was sorely tempted to marry him. He led the expedition to help the Dutch in 1585, and was given command of the English armies raised to resist a Spanish invasion; but he died, aged about fifty-six, in Armada year.

48

# What was the Spanish plan?

*The problem*    For King Philip, the obvious course of action was to mount a direct invasion of England. By conquering the country and deposing Queen Elizabeth, the Spaniards would defeat the enemy and incidentally solve at a stroke all their problems in the Netherlands and on the high seas. Even if they were wrong in believing that the majority of Englishmen were Catholics at heart and would welcome them with open arms, there was not much doubt that, once on English soil, Spanish troops could defeat any army their enemies could raise. English soldiers had already proved their fighting qualities in the Netherlands, but in the long run they could hardly hope to withstand the finest troops in Europe – the battle-hardened veterans commanded by the Duke of Parma. The problem, of course, was to establish Parma's army on English soil.

*The obstacle*    And what stood in the way were the finest ships in the world – the galleons of the navy which Henry VIII had laid down and which, under Queen Elizabeth, had been energetically expanded and improved over a period of ten years by John Hawkins. The chief characteristic of the galleon was that its keel was longer in proportion to its beam than in a merchant ship: that is, it was long rather than wide, making it more manoeuvrable and capable of mounting more guns to increase the devastation caused by its broadsides. Hawkins accentuated this feature, greatly reduced the size of the "towers" at the bow and stern (used for duels between soldiers rather than naval gunnery), and raised the deck level to accommodate even more guns. These royal galleons formed the nucleus of England's fighting force, though when war came their strength could be supplemented by volunteer and requisitioned vessels of various types. England's seamen, like Parma's soldiers, were veterans, blooded in their predatory descents on the Spanish Main. If King Philip needed any reminder of these unpleasant facts, it was provided by Drake, who in 1585-86 carried the war to the Spaniards: with a fleet of twenty-nine ships he captured and ransomed San Domingo and Cartagena, burned other Spanish settlements and even watered – and looted a little – off the coast of Spain itself.

*The solution?*    Philip's success in claiming the Portuguese throne made it

possible for him to contemplate a naval expedition against England. Whereas most Spanish vessels were designed for Mediterranean waters, the Portuguese had pioneered ocean-going ships and fighting galleons; though not as numerous or up-to-date as England's fleet, Portugal's formidable warships and experienced seamen were ultimately to provide the Armada with much of its fighting strength. Even so, Philip did not respond immediately to the invasion plan put forward by his navy chief, the Marquis of Santa Cruz, whose proposed Armada was so huge that it would have been beyond even Philip's resources. An alternative plan was put forward by Parma, who proposed a surprise attack across the Channel; it had the merit of being relatively cheap, since it involved ferrying 30,000 infantry and 4,000 cavalry to England overnight in flat-bottomed barges, with only twenty-five protecting warships. The objection to this was the difficulty of concealing such an operation – and the fact that if things went wrong the entire Spanish army would be wiped out. It seems to have been Philip himself who devised the final scheme, which combined elements from the other two: he would raise the largest fleet he could, and send it to rendezvous with Parma and escort his flat-bottomed barges safely across the Channel.

**The decision**    Preparations for "the Enterprise of England" went ahead, but it was by no means certain that Philip would decide to

*The execution of Mary, Queen of Scots, at Fotheringay Castle on 8th February, 1587. The picture uses a quaint story-telling technique, known as continuous representation, that was near obsolete in 1587. The Queen is shown three times in the same picture, entering the hall, being prepared for execution, and being decapitated.*

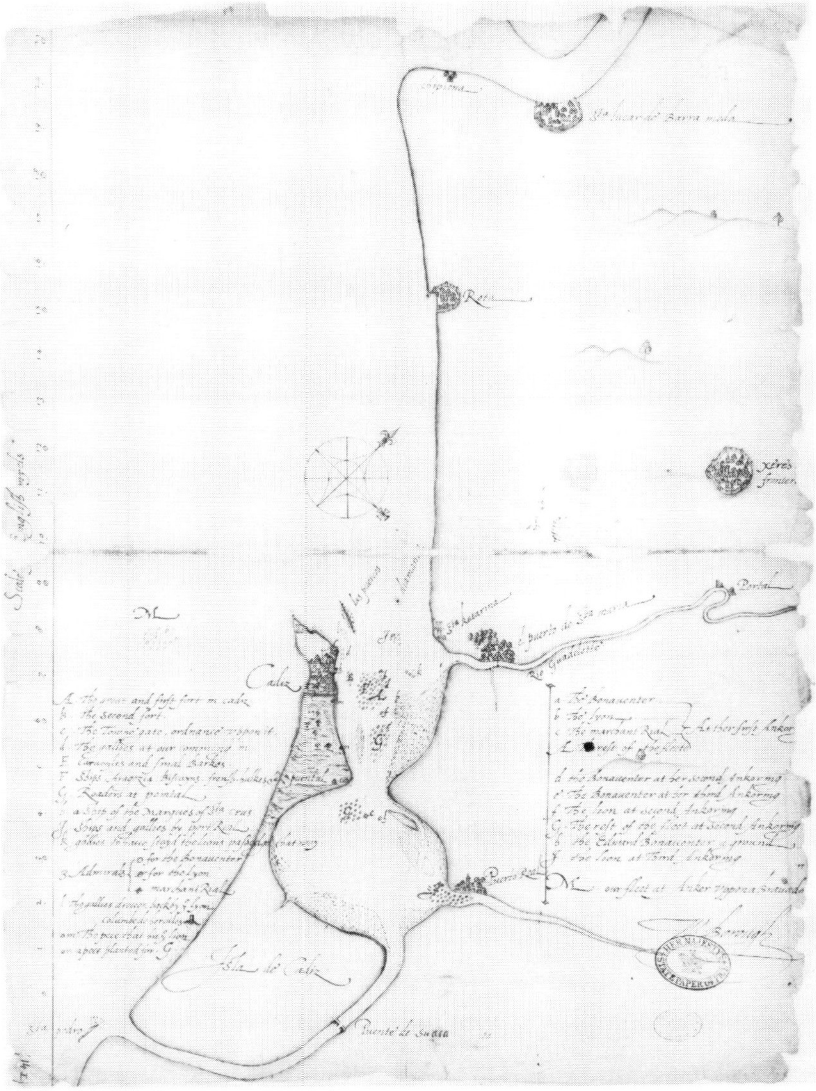

*Map of Cadiz, carried by William Borough, vice-admiral to Drake, during the raid in 1587 when Drake claimed to have "singed the King of Spain's beard".*

implement it. The event that seems to have made up his mind was the execution of Mary, Queen of Scots, on 18th February, 1587. Mary's connection with France had long ceased to be important, and she had increasingly counted on Spanish help in the various schemes for her liberation. Her will named Philip as her heir, so that for him the conquest of England became a holy, glorious and also self-interested task. Within a month he was acting with speed and impatience, accumulating ships, men, materials, victuals and equipment at Cadiz. His preparations were disrupted by Drake's famous raid on the port, when the Englishman "singed the King of Spain's beard", destroying quantities of stores and shipping.

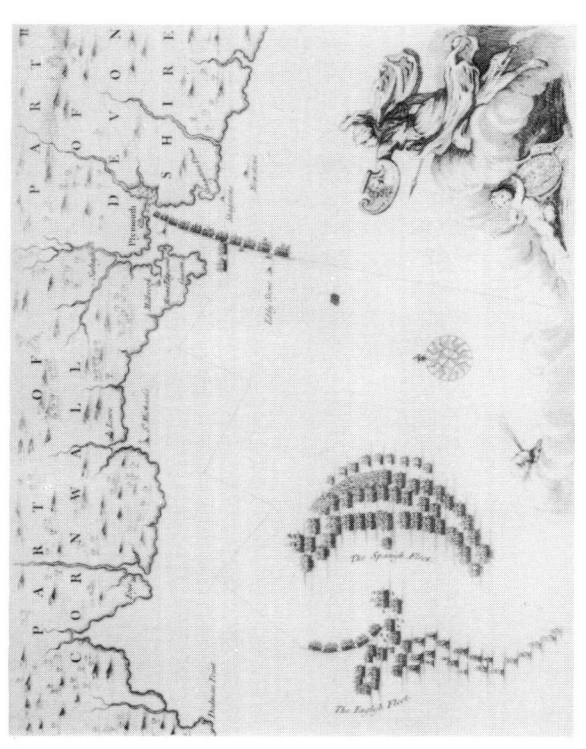

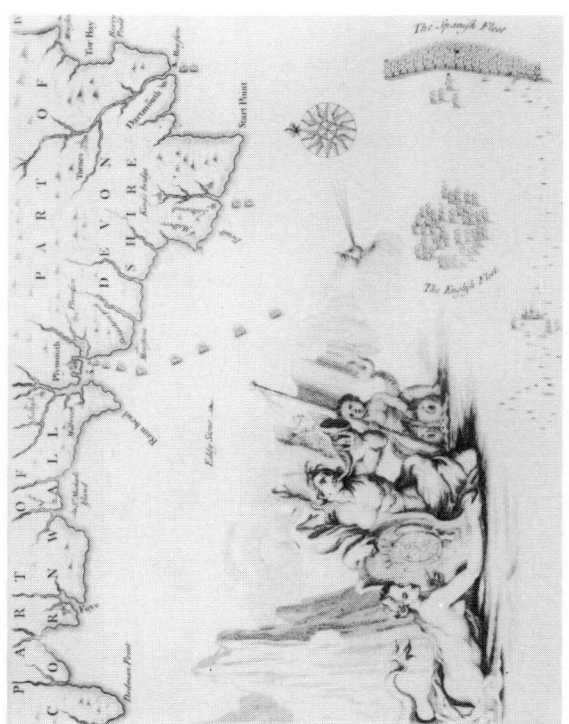

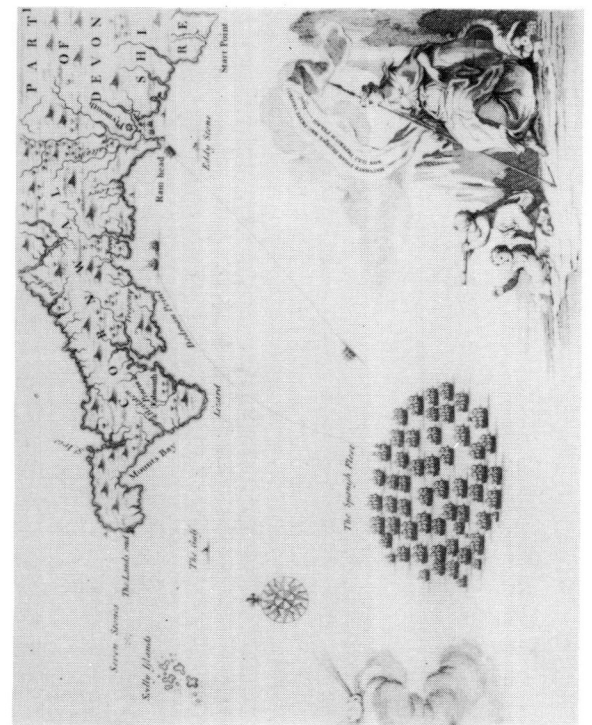

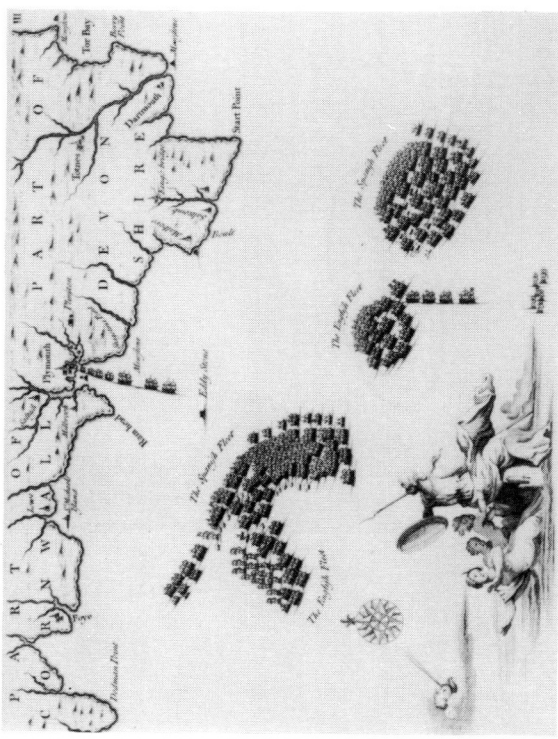

*The courses of the two fleets as they swept eastward through the Channel from the Lizard to the Kent coast. The maps are from John Pine's* Views of the Armada, *published in 1739. Pine derived his maps from those produced by Ryther (see picture on page 6).*

It took months to make good most of the damage, although the eager Philip pressed Santa Cruz to sail in mid-winter – an act that would have been suicidal if the Spanish admiral had not managed to stall the King from week to week. However, in February 1588 Santa Cruz died, and Philip appointed the Duke of Medina Sidonia in his place. The Duke was not a navy man, and not even much of a soldier: he was loyal and conscientious but, all too aware of his ignorance, felt unable to oppose the King's will in anything. It was Philip's good fortune that the man he appointed – mainly because he was a great nobleman – turned out to be a leader of some character and quite respectable abilities.

### Battling up the Channel

The delays irritated Philip, but they did give him time to bring off a coup that kept France out of the war. On 12th May, 1588, "the Day of the Barricades", the Spanish-subsidized Guise party staged an insurrection in Paris that effectively deprived the French king of his independence of action; if, now, the Spanish succeeded in invading England, there would be no question of France intervening to cut their lines of communication.

On the day before this, the Armada had at last set sail from Lisbon; but the fleet was almost immediately halted for a fortnight by contrary winds, and on 19th June it was forced back into Corunna by a storm. Then a change of wind urged it forward and drove back the English ships which had come out to seek the Spaniards. Arriving off the Lizard on 29th July, the Armada caught the English fleet re-provisioning in Plymouth harbour. Arguably the Spaniards might have sailed in and spread havoc, as Drake had done at Cadiz; this was certainly the course favoured by Recalde and other officers. But the Duke was bound by the King's instructions: the Armada was not to engage the enemy unless attacked, but was to concentrate on linking up with Parma. The Spaniards sailed on, shadowed by the English. The first clash occurred on 31st July, and there were three more in the course of the week. They were battles such as had never been seen before, involving huge quantities of powder and shot; and from an English point of view they were disappointingly inconclusive. The English outsailed their opponents, astonishing the Spaniards by their turns of speed and mastery of manoeuvre; but their gunnery was nothing like as effective as they had expected it to be. In theory, the far-firing culverins and demi-culverins on the English ships should have smashed the Spaniards without giving them a chance to reply; in practice they caused only light damage, mainly destroying rigging – which was fairly easily repaired – and killing some men. In the course of the week the Spaniards lost only three ships, more by accident than as a result of English gunnery. Spanish discipline was excellent, and the Armada maintained a tight formation that was very difficult to penetrate. Keeping together made its progress painfully slow, but meant that there were few stragglers for the English to pick off. The only cause for celebration on the English side was that the Spaniards had not dared to attempt a landing on the Isle of Wight, the last suitable point on the English coastline; and on Friday, 5th June Howard knighted Frobisher, Hawkins and others in recognition of their services against the would-be invader. Unknown to the English, the Duke of Medina Sidonia's instructions forbade him to attempt a landing on the English coast until he had tried to rendezvous with Parma. Obediently the Armada crossed the Channel and went to meet its destiny in Calais Roads.

# Could the Armada have succeeded?

*The element of chance* No one can give a firm answer to such a might-have-been question, but the facts are well-established enough to make some good guesses possible. We have already seen that the English were the better seamen and had better ships; but also that Spanish hulls and Spanish discipline were far stronger than their enemies expected. Could they have succeeded with a little more luck – if, say, the wind had blown in a different direction on the night of the fireships or during the battle of Gravelines? Luck has almost always played a part in war, and especially when the war was fought at sea, between wooden ships; even the finest ships and men were largely at the mercy of the winds and waves. The Armada had its fair share of good weather – notably during its progress up the Channel – but it might just have been luckier still. (There have been occasions when *everything* went right on a hazardous mission: a notable example was the Japanese plan to attack the US fleet in Pearl Harbor, described in another book in this series.) However, this raises another question: was the Armada scheme so ill-conceived that, with all the luck in the world, it could not possibly have succeeded? There seem to be good grounds for thinking that the answer is Yes.

*The inflexible plan* Both the English and the Spaniards would have given the action of the elements a different name: God's Will. Philip presented "the Enterprise of England" as a crusade: every man on board had to have a certificate testifying that he had confessed to a priest and received absolution; no women were allowed on the voyage (a rigorous search before launching revealed the presence of twenty, who were immediately ejected); and during it the men were forbidden to use blasphemous bad language. On the English side, the medal struck to celebrate victory said nothing about the navy: it carried the words *Flavit Jehovah et dissipati sunt*, "God breathed, and they were scattered". Philip II was so confident of God's favour that on occasion he referred to the *"Armada Invencibile"* – the "Invincible Armada", a catchphrase later seized upon by Protestant historians who wanted to highlight English heroism. Most of the Spanish leaders knew very well that the Armada was not invincible.

Philip's faith was one of the Armada's cruellest impediments. But for Santa Cruz, he would have sent it out into lethal mid-winter storms; and later he was to do just that with a subsequent armada. The certainty that God was on his side made Philip gloss over some of the difficulties of the enterprise, notably the liaison between the fleet and Parma's troops. And it encouraged his tendency to devise inflexible, seemingly God-given plans: Philip was by temperament a bureaucrat, ruling his empire by correspondence from an office in his palace, the Escorial in Madrid; he dictated or wrote many thousands of letters, giving distant subordinates detailed instructions about matters that might have been better left to those who were on the spot. Though he took note of plans and suggestions, he disliked the free play of debate, and there was never a round-the-table conference between the main Spanish participants in the Armada – an event that might have cleared up at least some of the misunderstandings between Medina Sidonia and Parma. Finally, as a God-inspired bureaucrat, Philip sent Medina Sidonia explicit instructions that made it impossible for the Duke to deviate from the King's plans in any circumstances. He was not to attack; so the chance of bottling up the English fleet in Plymouth was lost. And he was not to seize the Isle of Wight on the voyage out; so, despite Parma's worrying silence, the Armada left the last deep-water harbour it might have taken, and set out for a rendezvous that would have to be made in the face of the enemy and with no deep-water port to fall back on; for Parma did not control a single one. No one can be sure that the Spaniards would have succeeded in mauling the English fleet in Plymouth or in seizing the Isle of Wight, or even that they would have decided to so if they had had the chance. But it is certain that Philip's inflexibility made it impossible for them to react to changes in circumstance, and put them in a highly dangerous position, dependent for success on a single operation.

*A flaw in the plan*    Lack of a deep-water port accentuated the advantages enjoyed by the English as the defenders, fighting close to their home base. Above all, it was relatively easy for them to obtain reinforcements and fresh supplies. And so, although neither side foresaw the enormous quantities of ammunition they would expend in battle, it was the English who were able to make good the deficit; and that fact alone may have decided the battle of Gravelines. Without a suitable port, the Spaniards could not obtain fresh ammunition or replenish their victuals (though they did a certain amount of trade with the citizens of Calais). They had nowhere to wait in safety if

Parma was not ready to join them (he wasn't). And, when in difficulties, they had no place to repair their ships or even to take refuge in: that was why they had to undertake their long and disastrous voyage home round the British Isles. Lack of a deep-water port ensured that the Armada would be not only defeated but also shattered.

**The impossible task**  It also meant that the Armada could not go in to meet Parma: he and his men must rendezvous with the Spanish fleet in the Channel. This was the most serious flaw in the entire plan. Parma's barges were assembled at Dunkirk, but they were hemmed in by the flyboats of England's allies, the rebellious Dutch. The flyboats were small but fast and tough fighting ships; if Parma's barges – essentially shallow cattle-boats, without masts, sails or guns – tried to make their way out through the sandbanks outside Dunkirk, they and Parma's splendid army would be sitting targets. Even without the presence of the English fleet it is hard to imagine how the Spaniards could have got out: if the Armada had somehow defeated the English, it would still have been unable to enter the shallow waters round Dunkirk and dislodge the Dutch. In combination with the other facts we have noted, this makes it fairly safe to say that there was no way the Armada could have carried out its mission: the unlucky Medina Sidonia had been set an impossible task.

**Failures in communication**  This also appears to have been Philip's fault. Parma had warned him of the situation, and had suggested putting off the "Enterprise" until he could capture a deep-sea port such as Flushing. Philip had gone ahead, presumably believing that God would find a way. Most extraordinary of all was the fact that he had given no inkling of the difficulty to Medina Sidonia: all the instructions he issued implied that, if the Armada arrived, Parma would manage to come out. The Duke was so far misinformed that he thought Parma had his own fleet of flyboats, and on arriving at Calais he sent messages begging the general to let him have forty or fifty to help defeat the English. When one of his messengers returned to Calais Roads on Sunday, 7th August, and told him the real state of affairs, he must have been astounded, and perhaps realized for the first time that this huge, costly and hazardous expedition had been hopeless from the start.

**The role of Parma**  Parma's role in all this remains something of a mystery. His letters to Medina Sidonia were vague and evasive. He was supposed to be building flyboats and preparing barges, but the work went on slowly and met with innumerable obstacles – obstacles that we may be sure such a great man of action would have overcome if his heart had been set on doing so. And even when the Armada arrived at Calais Roads, he took his time about leaving his headquarters at Bruges for Dunkirk. Parma always insisted to the King that he had done everything he could, but he actually behaved as though he was playing for time, hoping the Armada would disappear before he was forced to act. Although Parma was no doubt aware of the hopeless nature of the Armada's mission, his behaviour made little sense, since his failure to build flyboats could only have made his chances even worse if he had been forced to emerge from Dunkirk; and no completely satisfactory explanation has ever been put forward. Perhaps it was less strange that on the night of Tuesday, 9th August, he suddenly began filling his sounder barges at Dunkirk with troops ready to embark. After all, he would later have to convince the exacting King Philip that he had really been willing to follow the royal plan; and it may be that by that date he was pretty sure the Armada had gone and would never return to Calais Roads.

*Alessandro Farnese, Duke of Parma, was the greatest soldier of his time. He commanded the Spanish army fighting the Dutch rebels, and was supposed to liaise with the Armada in the Channel. His slow preparations and politely unco-operative attitude have puzzled generations of historians.*

# The end of the Spanish threat?

*The cost of defeat*    Towards the end of 1588 the surviving ships of the Armada lay in Santander; and in the area around the port, Spaniards were still dying from the after-effects of their experiences on the voyage. Though estimates vary, it seems likely that about 60 ships had been lost out of the 130 that set sail from Lisbon, and many more must later have been written off as beyond repair. Of the Armada's 30,000 soldiers and sailors, as many as 20,000 may have perished. One writer estimates that about 1,500 died in battle, 6,000 were killed in shipwrecks, and 1,000 were murdered or executed in Ireland; the rest – that is, the majority – were victims of disease and malnutrition (which likewise killed more English sailors than the Spaniards did).

    The defeat of the Armada was also a political disaster. At a time when Catholicism seemed to be advancing on all fronts, Protestants everywhere were given new heart. The English victory meant that the Protestant party would retain control in Scotland, and that Dutch rebels and Huguenots would continue to receive English help; and as an early consequence of the Spanish setback, in December 1588 Henri III of France was emboldened to have the Duke of Guise assassinated and to reassert his authority. In France as in the rest of Europe, the struggle would go on, but the initiative was no longer so clearly with Spain.

*Spanish resurgence*    However, Spain remained the strongest single power in Europe, and her vast resources enabled King Philip to make good his naval losses with surprising speed. He concentrated on building up a fleet of ocean-going galleons of the type that had proved its worth during the Armada battles. The English did miss a chance of dealing the Spaniards a crippling blow while they were still stricken: in 1589 a large-scale expedition led by Drake and Elizabeth's best general, Sir John Norris, bungled their descent on the Portuguese coast and failed to capture Lisbon. After this, a resurgent Spanish navy became a formidable opponent, and there were no more easy English victories. The American historian Garrett Mattingly summed up the situation: "English sea-power in the Atlantic had usually been superior to the combined strengths of Castille and Portugal, and so it continued to be, but after 1588 the

margin of superiority diminished. The defeat of the Armada was not so much the end as the beginning of the Spanish navy." The Spanish treasure-fleets were more efficiently

◁ *Sir John Norris, England's best soldier, who distinguished himself during the Dutch Revolt and took part in the unsuccessful Portugal expedition.*

guarded, and more American silver reached Spain after 1588 than ever before. In 1595, when Drake and Hawkins once more set out to raid the Spanish Main, they found that here too the Spanish had learned the lessons of the past, fortifying their cities and carefully protecting their communications. The expedition proved a fiasco, and two great careers ended on a painful note of anti-climax when both leaders died during the voyage.

*The last fight of the Revenge, a famous incident from the post-Armada war years. In 1591 the Revenge, commanded by the ferocious Sir Richard Grenville, was surrounded by a Spanish fleet but fought on savagely until the ship was a total wreck and most of the crew were dead. Grenville, mortally wounded, was prevented by the few surviving crewmen from blowing up the ship, and finally surrendered after inflicting terrible damage on the Spaniards (four of their galleons eventually sank). The Revenge never reached port, going down in a storm with a number of its Spanish captors.*

### The last armadas

The English enjoyed one last triumph in 1596, when they sacked Cadiz and burned or captured the shipping in its harbour. This in turn provoked Philip to launch two more armadas in 1596 and 1597; but "God's breath", rather than the English, defeated them. The first, launched against advice into the autumn gales, had hardly left Spanish waters when it

The Anglo-Spanish peace conference, a momentous occasion recorded in this painting by Marcus Gheeraerts; the English chief minister, Robert Cecil, sits in the foreground, on the right. The war was ended by the Treaty of London, signed in August 1604.

was shattered and dispersed. The objective of the second was a landing at Falmouth, but it too was scattered by storms, though most of the Spanish ships did get safely back to port. Even Philip's death did not end the war; and in 1601 the Spaniards at last accomplished a successful landing – not on English soil but in Ireland, where the relatively small contingent of Spanish troops was compelled to surrender at Kinsale. After this the war tended to peter out. Philip III found it too expensive to pursue with vigour; and after the death of Queen Elizabeth in 1603, the new king – the pacific James I – hastened to make peace with Spain in August 1604.

# Further reading

## THE EVENTS

Winston Graham, *The Spanish Armadas*, Collins, 1972; Fontana paperback, 1976. A narrative covering the entire Anglo-Spanish war at sea.

Garrett Mattingly, *The Defeat of the Spanish Armada*, Cape, 1959, 1983. A classic account, relating the Armada to the wider political and diplomatic situation in Europe.

Stephen Underwood (editor), *The Great Enterprise*, Bell and Hyman, 1978. The story told entirely through contemporary documents.

David Howarth, *The Voyage of the Armada: the Spanish story*, Collins, 1981. The campaign seen from the Spanish point of view.

Niall Fallon, *The Armada in Ireland*, Stanford Maritime, 1978.

## THE INVESTIGATION

Many of the books already mentioned are also relevant here. Of the multitude of general works on the period, these are interesting and well-illustrated "starters":

Alison Plowden, *Elizabethan England*, Reader's Digest, 1982

Nathaniel Harris, *Spotlight on Elizabethan England*, Wayland, 1985

A.D. Ortiz, *The Golden Age of Spain 1516-1659*, Weidenfeld, 1971

Nathaniel Harris, *Spotlight on Renaissance Europe*, Wayland, 1986